RCL 20

RCL 20

People, Dreams & HP Calculators

Edited by W.A.C. Mier-Jędrzejowicz Ph.D. & Frank Wales

RCL 20: People, Dreams & HP calculators
Edited by W.A.C. Mier-Jędrzejowicz Ph.D. & Frank Wales

ISBN 0-9510733-3-8

Published by:
W.A.C. Mier-Jędrzejowicz
40 Heathfield Road
London, W3 8EJ
United Kingdom

British Library Cataloguing in Publication Data.
A catalogue record for this book is available from the British Library.

Printed and bound by Antony Rowe Ltd, Eastbourne, U.K.

CONTENTS

"HE SAYS HE'S DISCOVERED A NEW 'SYNTHETIC FUNCTION'."

Cartoon by Roger and Cathy Hill

Originally published in PPC Journal Vol. 8 No. 1
Reprinted with permission

Introduction

It is a very human thing to set up groups or clubs of people with a common interest. The rise of electronic equipment since the 1960s has provided many new opportunities for such clubs. One topic of interest was personal computing devices, and the first of these were hand-held programmable calculators.

The most successful club for users of these was PPC; this began in California and soon spread all round the world. This book celebrates 20 years of the club that was originally the British section PPC-UK, which later became the Handheld and Portable Computer Club, or HPCC.

Today, the term 'calculator' either conjures up the idea of 'adding machine', or those brightly-coloured devices sold in bubble-packs and intended for school and university mathematics work. But the kinds of calculators that were the focus of *our* club's attention were the *only* truly programmable and portable computers available to ordinary people. The programmability was key—it made them little software engines that could be applied to any task, not just mathematics. That they were still called 'calculators' belied their real capabilities—these machines were true portable computers, and are in many ways the ancestors of present-day laptops and PDAs.

This is not a history book; rather, it covers the first 20 years of HPCC through a series of recollections. The editors asked people associated with HPCC, and with HP handheld calculators or computers, for their recollections of those 20 years. That gave the book its title: "recall 20", or RCL 20 as it would appear in a program on an HP calculator.

Włodek Mier-Jędrzejowicz & Frank Wales
London, U.K.
September 2002

Book organisation

We have divided the book up into sections, each of which covers a topic concerning HPCC. Each section begins with an article by a member of HPCC, followed by articles related to that topic, by people who were friends—though not necessarily members—of HPCC.

Member IDs

Following the convention adopted by many clubs, we have put HPCC members' unique member IDs after their names in the titles of their articles.

English versus English

While the editors and some contributors live in Britain, many of the contributors live in the United States or elsewhere where idioms and the rules about spelling, grammar and punctuation are different from those of British English. So, where an American article might contain "color", "math", "flashlight", and capital letters after colons, a British one would contain "colour", "maths", "torch", and lower-case after a colon.

Rather than impose a single, "proper" style across all the articles, we have adopted a policy of editing according to the country of origin of the writer. This preserves the book's international flavour, and reflects the diversity and extent of the club and its members and friends.

Calculator Names

Hewlett-Packard have used various styles to represent their calculator product names in printed materials over the years: with an embedded hyphen (e.g., HP-35), with embedded space (e.g., HP 28), and all run together (e.g., HP30). As a result, we have all acquired varying and inconsistent habits when writing about them, none of which can be said to be more correct than any other. So, we have taken the cowardly decision to leave all calculator names as their authors have written them.

Acknowledgements

Many people contributed to this book. Most obviously, the authors who responded to our call, and wrote us many fine articles (several under fairly ridiculous deadlines that were entirely the editors' fault). Thank you all very much.

Our thanks to **Richard Nelson**, who made several things happen for us in the United States, and who effectively acted as our point man on the west coast. He also got us all started on this journey in the first place, by his efforts in creating PPC.

Thanks to **David Burch**, who got us started in the U.K., and managed to create something that continues today, despite his having let go of the reins a long time ago.

Our thanks to **Paola Kathuria**, who contributed an unreasonable amount of time, administration, design and technical expertise to make this book happen on time, and up to the standards we hoped we could attain. Thanks also to **T&D Limitless Web** for hosting the book project web site.

Finally, thanks to **Bill Hewlett** and **Dave Packard** for creating a company that was able to produce such incredible little computers, which have wrought changes in our lives out of all proportion to their size and modest specifications.

Contacting the editors

Włodek Mier-Jędrzejowicz   wlodek@hpcc.org

Frank Wales   frank@limov.com

Contacting HPCC

Information about HPCC is available from their web site: www.hpcc.org

You can also e-mail the Club Secretary: secretary@hpcc.org

RCL 20

WHY WE STARTED

It is worth recalling just how exciting the programmable calculators of the 1970s and 1980s were and why people set up clubs to discuss and use them. That excitement can be felt in the magazines and journals of the user clubs—or even reviews in mainstream computer journals. David Burch, founder of HPCC, shared that excitement. In this section, we reprint his original suggestion of setting up the club, and a rather special story that tied in to the same excitement, and extrapolated it into the future.

The original club, PPC, had its headquarters in southern Los Angeles, with local groups spread around America, Europe and Australia. They were called "Chapters" and had a measure of autonomy, but depended largely on PPC to provide a journal and contact with HP. The PPC Journal had a section "Chapter Notes" with news about local Chapters, and information from them. It was through Chapter Notes that PPC-UK was started.

The arrival of the HP-41 calculator with many new and powerful features had prompted a marked rise in the membership of PPC. One new member was so excited at discovering PPC that he wrote to the PPC Journal, suggesting that a British club should be set up. His letter appeared in PPC Journal, Volume 9, issue 2, in March 1982, in the "Chapter Notes" section. Here is that letter.

A LETTER TO PPC JOURNAL

MARCH 1982

DAVID BURCH (2)

Although having only recently joined PPC, the experience to date has been fantastic.

In January, awakened from sleep by a crash in my hall, I raced downstairs to find a 4.5lb parcel of PPCJ back issues had been pushed through my letterbox. Two hours later, still in my pyjamas and still sitting on the end of the stairs, I was becoming more and more confused by articles on NNN and Synthetic Programming. THEN, as we English say, "The penny dropped" - SOMEBODY HAD ACTUALLY FOUND A USE FOR THOSE STRANGE DISPLAY AND PRINTER CHARACTERS AND TEXT. Not only that, but at least 40% of the programs that I had spent hours and hours in writing, had already been written before - AND BETTER! - and were in PPCJ. Talk about re-inventing the wheel. So impressed am I that I enclose a plea for help via PPCJ.

HELP

I should like to contact other members in Britain who would be interested in exchanging experiences, ideas & programs with the ultimate objective of forming a full UK-Chapter of PPC. At present this is just a basic idea, but having talked to many HP-Users and Dealers, I'm convinced that there is a genuine demand. With the new HP-IL range of products, like Richard Nelson, I'm even more convinced that PPC and a UK-Chapter are needed. So, if you would be interested in joining, would like to help organize the chapter, or can only offer advice, then DO PLEASE CONTACT ME. (…)

David M. Burch (8267)

"Thank you, Beep...!" was published in issue 6 of the HP Personal Calculator Digest, in Summer 1978. In it, the well-known science fiction author, Gordon Dickson, wrote about a business traveller of the year 2038, and his HP handheld computer "Beep". We are now almost halfway between 1977 when the article was written, and 2038, the date when the story is set. Let us remind ourselves how exciting the future seemed, and how far along we are to the vision described in 1978. Our thanks to HP for their permission to reprint the article in this collection.

"Thank You, Beep...!"

Gordon Dickson

Walter Jensen, a middle-management executive in the year 2025, had just left a meeting in Tahiti, and was on his way to a conference in London, England, hand-carrying some very secret and valuable commercial information. He had taken a short-hop shuttle from Tahiti to Melbourne, Australia, and there caught the sub-orbital flight from Melbourne to London. The day had been a long one, and the pressures of business in the twenty-first century were severe. He sank into his seat compartment aboard the sub-orbital rocketliner of Pacificon Flight number 859 with a sigh of relief. Closing his eyes, he dozed off.

He woke with a start some time later, to find the rocketliner jarring to a landing. The vision screen before his seat showed an unfamiliar airport, dark with night and rain. This was not England. He buzzed for a steward and a neatly mustached face under a uniform cap appeared on the screen before him.

"Our apologies to our passengers," said the seat speaker. "A malfunction has aborted flight 859. We are now landing at the airport in Jakarta, Indonesia. Would you please proceed to the terminal, where schedule adjustments and other arrangements can be made?"

The rocketliner ceased moving. Walter snatched up his portfolio and stumbled out with the other passengers.

The crowd turned right into a wide corridor, and still thick with sleep, Walter followed them.

As he went, he began to awaken; and after some little distance he became aware that he had become separated from the others. He was alone in the corridor, with advertising signs in a language he could not read.

A small, slim man with golden skin and an oriental fold over his eyes, came hurrying by in the opposite direction.

"Say," said Walter, stepping in the other's path. "Could you tell me—"

But the other only rattled briefly at him in some unfamiliar language, then hurried out of sight. Walter was left alone, lost in an airport terminal he had never seen before.

He fumbled in his pockets, but without finding what he searched for.

"Beep!" he said, desperately, "Beep, where are you?"

A soft, musical tone sounded from his portfolio. Walter opened it and fished out an instrument looking like a slim, handheld calculator, with the upper third of its surface a vision screen. As soon as the heat of his hand enfolded it, the tone stopped; and the instrument, his Hewlett-Packard XX2050 autosecretary, spoke to him.

"What can I do for you, Walter?"

Its voice had, by Walter's choice, been factory-set to the same range as that of the voice of his wife, Enid. It was not Enid's voice, however, but a similar, cheerful, impersonal one he had come to identify with the code name Beep.

"I'm lost. Beep," Walter said now. "My flight aborted. I'm somewhere in a terminal at Jakarta, Indonesia. Also, I'm out on my feet, and I don't know where to go, and how do I get to London now in time for tomorrow's conference?"

"Don't concern yourself, Walter," said the HP-XX2050. "I'll take care of everything. Tell me, do you see any tie-in computer consoles near you?"

Walter looked up and down the corridor.

"No."

"Very well then. I'll scan and locate some for you. Follow the arrow, please."

Walter looked down and saw an image of the corridor on the screen of the XX2050—with a glowing arrow pictured as lying on the floor just before him. As he stepped forward, the arrow moved ahead at him, pointing the way he should go.

He followed it for some distance down the corridor, and up a branching one. It led him finally into a carpeted area, where half a dozen comfortable chairs sat facing tables holding vision screens. He sat down at one of the tables and slid the HP- XX2050 into a slot in the tabletop. The large screen before him lit up with the concerned face of a clean-shaven middle-aged man.

"Mr. Jensen!" said the console, in slightly accented English. "Your autosecretary is now in contact with all local service computer nets. Our apologies for finding yourself astray in our terminal. If you'll wait where you are for just a minute or two, well send a vehicle for you. Would you care for anything in the way of food or drink at this time?"

"Not right now," said Walter, heavily. "I just want some sleep."

"Your autosecretary has already been put in touch with local hotel services," said the speaker. "Unfortunately, there're no further flights to London tonight, but a booking has been made for you on a rocketliner leaving tomorrow at ten a.m.. As soon as you clear customs, you'll be brought to a hotel room, selected on information from your autosecretary as to your personal taste."

"Good," said Walter, closing his eyes.

The familiar musical tone jerked him back from the sleep be had begun to fall into immediately.

"Oh. Sorry, Beep." He reached out and took the XX2050 out of its slot, placing it in his shirt pocket.

"Everything's taken care of, Walter," it said to him from the pocket. "I made all the necessary arrangements through the local computer networks. But don't fall asleep again. Your transportation will be here in five seconds."

"Five seconds?" But Walter had already heard the whisper of blowers, and a small, two-seater automated personnel carrier slid up to him, floating on the cushion of air from its underbody fans.

"If you'll take a seat, Mr. Jensen," the carrier said. "I'll bring you directly to the customs area."

Walter grunted an acknowledgment, got up and climbed into the nearest of the two seats. The vehicle moved off. In no time at all, it turned in through a doorway and stopped before another table with a vision screen.

"Slot me, Walter," the HP-XX2050 instructed him from the shirt pocket.

He fumbled it out and slid it into the slot provided. The screen lit up with the smiling face of a young lady.

"Mr. Jensen! Sorry we lost you earlier. Your luggage is already through custom check and passed on to the cab rank. Would you place your portfolio on the table, please?"

Walter did so. There was a faint hum for a moment.

"Very good, sir. Now, if you'll just give us your thumbprint. Thank you, you are now cleared through customs. We hope, in spite of the unscheduled nature of your stay in Jakarta, that you find matters here to your comfort."

"Yes. Well..." began Walter, taking back his portfolio. But his vehicle was already moving him off through glass doors into a pleasant tropical night, where an aircushion automated taxi waited at the curb. He woke with the stopping of the cab some little time later to find himself once more at the curbside. A live doorman—evidence of a luxury hotel—

opened the cab door. "Mr. Jensen!" he said. "Your room is ready, sir. If you'll step through the doors ahead, you'll find a bellcart waiting to take you to it."

"Thanks," said Walter. Clutching the portfolio, he went in and took a seat in the bellcart—an aircushion vehicle not unlike the one that had transported him in the terminal. Three minutes later, it slid him through automatically opening doors into his room.

"Ah!" said Walter exhaustedly, collapsing in the nearest overstuffed chair. A glass in which ice tinkled was sitting on a table at his elbow. He sipped gratefully from it.

"I trust the drink is to your liking, sir," said a speaker grille in the wall of the room.

"Fine. Just right," said Walter.

"And would you want something to eat, Mr. Jensen?"

"Yes. Something simple. Clam chowder and a chicken sandwich."

"Yes sir. If I might get the details from your autosecretary…?"

Walter took the HP-XX2050 from his pocket, and looking around, discovered a slot in the table at his elbow. He inserted the XX2050.

Forty minutes later, having called home, and climbed into a luxurious, air-cushion bed, Walter was sleeping soundly. Meanwhile the XX2050, in the slot of a bedside table, was silently beaming calls to London, to make sure that the next day there would go smoothly. It wound up with an electronic note to itself to wake Walter—who was a slow starter—an hour and a half before he was due to board his flight, and then switched itself into a wait-state.

The XX2050, of course, did not stop to be impressed by the number of things it could do to make Walter's life easier, and Walter himself, by this time, also took its services for granted.

He was, in fact, electronically pampered to a degree that was beyond the imagination of his ancestors. What made it all possible was the remarkable advances in computer science since the late twentieth century, plus a society geared to the use of such technological tools.

His portfolio, lying on a chair while he slept, contained information in a form as rare, nowadays, as the information itself. The form was that of printouts from the computer of the branch of Walter's company in Tahiti. Ordinarily, Walter did not see a piece of paper from one year's end to the next, any more than he normally had to deal personally with the multitude of government and other forms that influenced his life. All such things were handled for him now by the computers of the world, to which his XX2050 was an access point.

In very real fact, as long as he had the XX2050, he needed very little else in the way of material things. The XX2050 was like a latter-day Aladdin's lamp, which could summon up anything be needed and that either he or his company could afford. It did this by interlocking with the large, established computer nets wherever it happened to be, just as it had here in Jakarta.

When Walter had first found himself lost in the terminal, the XX2050 had used its built-in receiver to pick up a broadcast signal directing them to the nearest terminals of the airport computer net, translating the signal into a moving arrow of light on its screen for Walter's benefit. It could, if necessary, also have directed him to the computer terminals by voice directions.

Once slotted in one of the terminals, the XX2050 had been in direct connection with the airport computer net; and it had immediately contacted Pacificon Airline for a future flight, and discussed the clearing of Walter's luggage with customs.

The airport computer net was, of course, interconnected with all the other public service nets of the Jakarta area. Through the net dealing with the autotaxis, the XX2050 had arranged for a cab to take Walter to this hotel, and through the hotel/motel network, had arranged for the sort of room Walter preferred. Finally, it had given the hotel computer full instructions on Walter's choice of food and drink, so that the clam chowder and the chicken salad sandwich were made and seasoned to his personal taste.

The relationship of the XX2050 to the computer nets in Walter's work and personal life was no less intricate. It was like a staff of personal secretaries, switchboard operator, and personal business manager, combined.

Aside from the nets, all by itself, the XX2050 had some remarkable capabilities. In its slim shape it possessed a gigabyte of memory power. Also, it had the ability to transmit and receive on a number of frequencies, including a pulsed signal that could alert a special response in one of the communication satellites overhead at all times in orbit around the Earth.

But such communication was for emergency situations. Most was of the direct slot-connection type. Next most common was short-range air-wave talk with other computer nets, including those of the international telephone networks. The XX2050 could open safes, lock up or unlock offices and houses, translate for Walter in the basic vocabularies of over fifty different languages, or teach him to speak a new one. It had been programmed with a number of systems, including one that allowed it to operate as a watchdog over Walter's general health, and give instructions about him, in a medical emergency, to any adult human nearby—such as in the case of a dangerous reaction to any one of the several allergies that Walter possessed.

Aside from this, the HP-XX2050 also received information from a number of sensors which had been implanted in Walter's body to keep track of everything from his blood pressure to indications of infection. Not only did it keep a running record for Walter's doctor, it could also, in case information from the sensors warranted it, warn Walter if certain food and drink was unwise for him, advise him when it was necessary to rest, or even call aloud for help in an emergency situation.

With all this care being taken of people like Walter, it might be questioned what inhabitants of the mid twenty-first century would do

with all the spare time that their autosecretaries gained for them.
Unfortunately, as Walter himself had discovered, the more you had
time to do, the more that was found for you to do; which was probably
one of the reasons the world was enjoying a per-capita productivity
nowadays several times that which would have been considered possible,
fifty or a hundred years before.

Nonetheless, cared for in this fashion Walter slept soundly, without
worries. On waking, he found what he would have ordered himself for
breakfast, already laid out and waiting for him.

So pleasant, in fact, was breakfast, after the events of the previous day,
that he lingered over it longer than he normally would have, in spite of
the warnings of the XX2050, and ended by having to rush to make his
substitute flight, after all. Safe at last in the stratosphere and London-
bound at nearly five thousand miles an hour, he relaxed and fell into
conversation with a marine archaeologist in the opposite seating
compartment, who had just finished six months of research at a station
on the bottom of the Mindanao Trench, nearly seven miles beneath the
surface waves of the Philippine Sea.

So interesting was this conversation that it was not until the plane had
landed and he was climbing into an autocab that a nagging sense of
something wrong surfaced in the shape of a sudden realization.

"Beep!" he said. "My portfolio! I forgot to take it when we left the
hotel this morning. It's still there, back in Jakarta; and I'm due in an
hour at the conference. The minute I get there those have to be read
into the records of everyone there."

"It's all right, Walter," said the XX2050. "The hotel messaged the
airport as we were taking off, to report the portfolio had been left
behind. I gave directions to put it on a cargo rocket leaving right after
us. It's a completely automated cargo rocket, and scheduled to operate
at trans-human accelerations. So it landed an hour and a half before us,
and your portfolio is already at the conference site. You can pick it up
from the Credentials Desk as you go in."

"Oh," said Walter. He sank back in his seat, wiping a suddenly damp brow. "Good. Very good. Thank you, Beep...!"

"My pleasure, Walter," said the HP-XX2050, primly.

How we started

The letter from David Burch brought a quick response from other British members of PPC, and the business of setting up PPC-UK got under way. Richard Nelson, who had started the original PPC provided help and advice, but the work was done by the enthusiasts in Britain. Right from the beginning, David's idea was that PPC-UK would be more than just a local chapter of PPC—he wanted to cover the whole of the country. Early meetings bore this out—they were held in Lechlade, Leeds, and points between. After several such meetings, and a great deal of work, PPC-UK was up and running.

When collecting articles for this book, we talked with David about the setting up of PPC-UK, and what he thinks of the club 20 years on. David points out that new members came not just from PPC, but also from readers of HP's magazine, Key Notes.

THE FOUNDING OF HPCC

AN INTERVIEW WITH DAVID BURCH (2)

FRANK WALES (3)

Frank Wales talks with David Burch, the founder of the HPCC, about forming the club.

FRANK: *It's been twenty years since you founded PPC-UK, which eventually became HPCC. Are you surprised that it's still going?*

DAVID: Yes, but I'm also glad it is. I still think of the club as my baby, even though I haven't been involved now for a long while. The club came about at a time when people were still "exploiters" of machines—they loved to open the bonnet and tinker, to see how it worked, and even to add go-faster stripes. These days, people just tend to be users rather than exploiters, and don't lift the bonnet any more.

Assuming they even know it's there.

Exactly. To a certain extent, the world has moved on from when I formed the club.

Plus, HP's machines were self-contained little development environments—you didn't have to spend nine-hundred bucks to get the development system for a PC just to write a little program.

Indeed.

Clearly, you picked the right people, and established the right principles, to create something that has endured. What was the biggest challenge in bringing the club about?

Making contact with enough people. Henry Horn and *HP Key Notes* turned out to be critical to getting the club off the ground.

Why was that? Didn't your letter to PPC *Journal produce a good response?*

PPC Journal's readership was mainly people who were already the "under the bonnet" types, and who knew where to find things out. *Key Notes* reached the ordinary user of HPs, and that was what was needed to create the critical mass for the club to be a success.

The other challenge was trying to establish what people wanted from the club.

Having said all that, yes, you're right about picking the right people. I was lucky to get the initial group I did, people who were infectious, who would be able to take things forward afterwards. I remember giving Włodek a lift one evening, and said to him: "before long, you'll be running the club." And before long, he was!

The first meeting was at Graeme [Cawsey]'s house in Lechlade, I think, then another one a week after in Crawley. John French and Włodek were at both of those, I think. Did you come to those?

No, my first meeting was at Zengrange in Leeds.

That was probably the third meeting.

What surprised you the most in setting the club up?

The amount of interest and dedication that people showed towards handhelds.

Why did you decide to produce a magazine right from the start?

I thought it was going to be the only way to keep the club alive. If it was just conferences and meetings, I didn't think it would last.

And why did you decide to organise a conference so quickly after the start of the club?

I had this in mind almost from the beginning. I felt the club had to start with a bang. If it just rolled slowly along, it would never have succeeded in the long run. I also spoke to a few people here and in Europe, and they all wanted a conference of some kind. I remember spending hours on the phone to you, and figured a conference might cut my phone bill down a bit.

What do you remember particularly about that first conference?

I remember that I didn't get to hear any of the talks, I was rushing around so much. I don't think I was even in attendance at the talks I gave. I've always been useless at delegating, and anyway, there were so many things that I had to do. I didn't plan enough spare time, and people over-ran their allotted slots.

I remember being scheduled to give a one-hour talk on extended functions, from 11am to midday or something, and everyone before over-ran so much, I ended up with ten minutes to give my presentation, and I was the last one before lunch. I ended up whizzing through, and saying: "see me later for more details." Enough people came back in the evening that I ended up spending two hours talking, so it all still worked out okay.

Yes, I remember how enthusiastic everyone was; people were turning up without having bought a ticket. One person called at the last minute from Sweden, I think, to see if he could still attend.

Looking back, are you glad you spent the time and effort on it that you did? Was it all worth it?

Yes. It brought about a complete change of direction for my life, and indeed others. One aspect is how many people the club helped, providing them with a stepping-stone to other careers. You, Graeme, Julian, other people who got hired by Zengrange, for example. It's pleasing to know that you've helped other people—that sounds so mushy when you say it that way, but anyway.

Part of your motivation in forming the club was to have like-minded people available who might have solved problems that you encountered, and to compensate for poor support and information availability.

Yes.

Given the growth of the net, and the way people now use it, what role do you think clubs like HPCC will have in the future?

To be honest, I'm not sure that they will have a role, given HP's current apparent dislike of calculators.

If you take a look online, though, there are clearly still people gathering at web sites with discussion areas, talking about what they're doing now, and not just what things were like in the "Good Old Days." Perhaps the future of things like Datafile *is more online, and less subscription-based?*

Please don't misunderstand me; I'd love the club to continue for a long time yet, but I'm just not sure, with such new machines as there are being more user-oriented rather than exploiter-oriented, I think there's less impetus to play with them, and fewer people with the enthusiasm for playing.

Thanks for taking the time to talk today, David.

You're welcome.

The HP calculators, and the user clubs, did more than excite people—they changed our lives. Frank Wales reminisces about what HP calculators and PPC-UK meant to him.

I BLAME BILL & DAVE

FRANK WALES (3)

I could have been a doctor, you know, if it hadn't been for Bill Hewlett and Dave Packard. It's all their fault that I don't routinely examine other people's bowels or get asked at parties about odd-looking growths.

Let me explain.

There I was, in the summer break between the first and second years of medical school, when I picked up the September 1979 special issue of *Scientific American* on 'The Brain'. Little did I suspect that an advertisement inside would change my future. It had the headline: "A Calculator. A System. A Whole New Standard." It was for the HP-41C, HP's new block-buster calculator. It was not only programmable, it also had *peripherals*. It had a printer, it had a magnetic card reader that could store data and programs on little strips of plastic, it accepted modules that added memory or software written by other people, and it even had a bar code wand! Holy moley, what was *that* for? And, wait a minute, it had a white display that could show *letters* as well as numbers, an alphabetic keyboard, a facility to customise what each button did, the ability to give programs *names* and have as many of them in the machine at once as would fit, *and* it remembered everything for as long as you wanted, even if you switched it off.

Well, at this point I was light-headed. I'd been using calculators for years, and had amassed a small collection as I'd gone through school. Programmability had come along in my last year, and I'd gone through the *Sinclair Scientific Programmable* (capable of storing a program up to 24 steps long), the *Sinclair Cambridge Programmable* (36 steps in a smaller case), and had acquired a mighty Texas Instruments TI-58 when I went to university, which was sleek, black, angular and could store 480 steps (but unfortunately forgot them all when it was turned off). But seeing the HP-41C ad was like being someone who'd had a couple of bicycles and a scooter, and who was presently driving around in a Ford Escort, only to discover that there was this little company called Mercedes-Benz.

I had been toying with the idea of getting one of the so-called *personal* computers that had been showing up around this time, but things like the Commodore PET, the TRS-80 and the Apple II all had two problems: they were too expensive, and they were tied to mains power. I really wanted a computer that I could carry around with me, rather than one that stayed at home. I wanted one because I secretly enjoyed programming a lot more than my "official" studies, and I wanted to learn more about software. I was also successfully deluding myself that I could have a day-job in health care, and just do programming in my spare time (of which I would have approximately zero hours per week for the next hundred years). The appearance of the HP-41C effectively put paid to that little scenario, although I didn't realise it right away.

I had to have one, and months of waiting for them to appear at the local calculator shop only heightened my anticipation. It didn't help that, in the interim, I'd become fed up with the short-comings of the TI-58 (losing all the programs and data when switched off, clunky user interface, rattly keyboard) and had sold it and bought an HP-33C, an entry-level little machine. This really sealed my fate, because it let me discover just why HP calculators were considered in a different league from all the other machines on the market:

- the build quality was amazing—it felt *just right* in the hand; the keyboard had a fabulous tactility to it that was almost seductive to use, and the whole thing just seemed like it would last longer than me

- its *Reverse Polish Notation* system, with its four-level stack and **last-x** was just *so obviously* better than the alternative "algebraic input" (yeah, right) systems of its competitors—it let you back up, correct errors, change your mind as you worked through a problem, and let you see the answer take shape as you went along, so you could have confidence in it

- errors didn't blow away what you were working on—you could clear them and continue from where you had got to before doing the wrong thing, as opposed to the lame, lazy behaviour of other machines where a blinking 'E' meant you had to start again

- it had a whole gamut of carefully thought-out functions and operations that clearly provided a cohesive set of capabilities—it didn't have all that bolted-on statistics rubbish, or the collection of disjoint function sets amusingly called "modes", that are the hallmark of badly designed machines—it even had built-in self-tests that you could use to prove it was still working okay!

- it looked good too—it was clearly a serious tool for serious work, and even people who didn't ordinarily care about such technology were drawn to look at it, to touch it, to pick it up and to ask about it

Despite being merely a little computational device, it had a physical and a logical design that set it apart from all the other products ostensibly like it on the market. It had clearly been designed and manufactured under the supervision of people who: a) knew what they were doing, and b) actually cared about putting the best possible tool in the hands of the customer.

Given that this entry-level calculator—this mass-produced widget—was of such obviously high quality, what could HP's new top-of-the-line machine be like? I couldn't resist. I had to have one.

Being a poor student, I had to take out an HP loan[1] to buy the HP-41C that I had ordered. It arrived at the end of 1979, and it is perhaps no coincidence that my academic performance went south shortly thereafter. I found myself looking forward to my next laboratory assignment, not because I wanted to learn more about the biochemical or pharmaceutical principle it was meant to be teaching me, but because it gave me the chance to write yet *another* purposeful program on my HP-41 to solve the problems posed in the experimental notes. My fellow students became interested when they saw that I was able to complete the work faster and more accurately than they could, thanks to the programs I was writing before and during each lab. It wasn't long before it was routine in labs for me to pass my HP-41 around the bench for everyone else in my group to use for their calculations and reporting as well. But this also meant I had to take the time to make sure the program was correct, and that it could be used by people who didn't have a clue about things like *RPN*.

Without realising it, I had become an end-user application programmer in a vertical market, and was spending more of my time at the back of lectures writing software for the next lab than paying attention to the boring noise coming from the front of the lecture hall. That I found my "real" studies boring is possibly the largest single clue that I had got on the wrong train, academically speaking, but it wasn't until I started meeting real patients in actual hospitals that the penny dropped that I was in the wrong place. Then it was merely a case of breaking my parents' hearts, annoying my tutors and making most of my friends think I was a total idiot by bringing to a conclusion the chain of events that were put into motion when I saw that advert in *Scientific American* a year before—I stopped attending classes, got kicked out of medical school, then immediately went back and signed up for computing science, and got a real education in the stuff I'd been figuring out in my "spare time."

---

[1] In fact, the type of loan I took out is called "hire purchase", where you make regular payments, but the item is legally only on hire to you from the loan company until the final payment is made, at which point you have *actually* purchased it. This type of scheme is generally referred to by its initials: HP. I am not making this up.

It was during this second wind of studies that I found out about PPC. This also happened as a result of one of the more subtle qualities of the Hewlett-Packard Company—after-sales support. *For calculators!* HP published a little magazine called *HP Key Notes* that printed useful information, tips and other things of value to their calculator customers. The December 1980 issue printed a review of a book by a certain Dr William Wickes called "Synthetic Programming on the HP-41C". If that isn't a title designed to pique the interest, I don't know what is. What on earth was *synthetic* programming?[2] I ordered a copy of this book, which described how to do entirely new and undocumented jiggery-pokery on the very machine that I thought I knew pretty well by this point. It also revealed an amazing amount of information on how the 41 worked internally, none of which I had had access to before.

The book also explained about this group you could join, to learn more and even be a part of the process of discovery: PPC in Santa Ana, California. I joined up, bought all the back issues of the *PPC Journal* back to the release of the HP-41, and was as happy as a pig in the proverbial. There was so much to learn, and almost all of it was useful, either directly in programs I was writing, or as practical examples for my studies.

In March 1982, David Burch's letter appeared in *PPC Journal*, inviting people in the U.K. to contact him to help set up a British chapter of PPC—the rest, as they say, is the history that's written down elsewhere in this book. Through what was started as PPC-UK, and what has since become HPCC, I met John French (who ran Zengrange), who

---

[2] Okay, I'll tell you. It's programming the calculator using instructions that the designers didn't anticipate you could enter. They come about by playing tricks on the machine to glue together bits and pieces of instructions in its memory. It will then blithely execute these, on the assumption that they must make sense. This process of synthesising new instructions from existing parts gives "synthetic programming" its name. On the HP-41, synthetic programming had so many benefits that enormous amounts of effort went into making it easier. I'm proud to say that one of my contributions to this art was co-developing ZENROM, which eliminated the distinction between synthetic programming and regular programming.

subsequently hired me and some other PPC-UK members to develop cool stuff for what today would be called the "HP-41 computing platform" and its successors. Those people had all seen what was great about HP calculators, and had absorbed some of the values of HP as a result. Over the next several years of working with and for HP, we learned a career's worth of lessons on how to design systems, how to treat customers and how to use technology, lessons that still serve us well many years after having left Zengrange for other computing pastures.

Bill Hewlett once said that HP calculators were ambassadors of HP quality, and he was right. However, they also carried the virus of HP values, able to infect susceptible individuals, and lure them into thinking that excellence and high quality are worthwhile and attainable, and worth striving for.

I never had the pleasure of meeting Bill or Dave while they were alive. I always imagined that, if I had, I would have said: "it's *your* fault I'm not a doctor, and for that I'd like to shake your hand."

Even before we had discovered the excitement of using a powerful handheld calculator, people in the USA had been making the same discovery, and finding ways to become owners of these expensive devices.

THE MOST TOYS

ABOUT THE BEGINNINGS OF MY HP EXPERIENCE

DEAN LAMPMAN

In 1972 I was working as chief project engineer for "The French Oil
Mill Machinery Co." when I opened up IEN (*Industrial Equipment News*)
and saw a calculator that would do trigonometric functions. We had a
number of trig. table books and there was always someone looking up
values to do gear force calculations, including myself.

I had authority to buy things up to $500 for the department and the
HP35 price was $495. So I filled out a company request and walked it
down to purchasing. (I wanted one of these things *now*.) When I handed
the req. to Tom (our purchasing agent), he looked at it and said: "NO
WAY, LAMPMAN, YOU'RE TRYING TO BUY A TOY. HAVE AL SIGN IT OR I
WON'T BUY IT." [For background information: 'Al' is Al French, the
owner of a $26-million-a-year Machinery Design and Build
Corporation, who, by the way, was an MIT mechanical engineer (M.E.).]

Since I wanted it that bad, I walked straight to Al's office and showed
him the ad, and was ready to defend my request with logic and cost and
speed and accuracy, etc.. He looked up at me and said: "Get two—I
want one," and then he took the requisition and changed the *1* to *2* and
handed it back to me.

I ran to Tom's office and put it right it front of him on his desk. He
said: "I don't believe you, there wasn't even enough time for you to get
there and back." So he picked up his phone and dialed Al and said:
"Lampman's in here trying to buy toys and using your name because it
is over his allowable limit." I wish I knew what was said on the other
end, because his face turned beet red and then he said: "Yes, Sir," and
slammed the phone down. He looked at me with daggers and said: "You

set me up." I was going to say I was sorry—then one of those out-of-the-blue ideas hit me. I said: "Sure did. Now you have to call the order in instead of mailing it, and you have to have it shipped UPS instead of mail, or I will go in every morning and ask Al if he got his yet because I haven't seen mine."

I don't remember if it was Monday or Tuesday when I ordered it, but I do remember the Friday at 10am that I got it. It went home with me all weekend and I spent over four hours a day Saturday and Sunday learning RPN. When I came in on Monday, Al wanted to be tutored and I was ready. We got to be fast friends because we were the Two High-Tech Engineers who knew RPN and stacks and memory.

Since I was going to grad school for my Masters in Operations Research, I had the 35 in my pocket all the time. Well, one day in FORTRAN class we were doing complex expression evaluations, and the professor was explaining how the stack was used, *and the light went on— WOW!* HP was going to make the 35 *programmable*; that was why it used RPN.

So—the next morning when I got to work, the very first thing I did was get the 35 warrantee card and dictate a letter that said: " I know you are going to make the 35 programmable and I want one of the first ones." I figured I would wait a week and if there was no answer, I would call.

Two days later, I get a call from Dick Bauman who starts out: "Are you an M.E., what would an M.E. want to program?" After I started going on in great detail, he interrupted and said: "Can you sign a non-disclosure agreement?" I said: "Sure," and he said he couldn't talk until he got it back and hung up. I got it UPS the next day, so I took it in and told Al that I was going to sign it, and he insisted that the lawyers OK it first. So we all had lunch at the country club, and I mailed it back that day.

Three days later, my wife calls me at work and says the UPS won't let her sign because it was for me only. So I told her to feed him, or sit on him, or chain him to the door knob, but do not let him leave. I was driving a '62 Vette at the time, and on the way home I learned that you can run a Vette 500 RPM over red-line. When I opened up the package, it was an HP65 and a letter asking for samples of what an ME might write programs for.

So off to school I go, *hi ho, hi ho!* The HP35 owners were an exclusive club, and we got together three times a week to trade techniques and meet new joiners. The first night I had it at school, there were ten people who had learned how to program it and store the program on a card. That turned out to be a big problem, since I only had five cards. That was all HP had sent, because they were still trying to perfect putting iron oxide on a small piece of plastic.

By the next night at school, everyone who could program had a 100-step program, and they wanted a card for it, and we wanted the programs for each of us also. The following meeting we had about five rolls of computer mag tape from the tape drives that everyone had at work. We compared the colors of the oxides, and determined that the low-density tape was the same color. Then out came a Swiss Army pocket knife with scissors, and we made a piece of tape the same dimensions as the HP card. Well, it would not feed because it was too thin. When everyone left to go home that night, you would have thought that they were leaving a funeral.

The next night, we had some cards that were made by using two pieces of tape and rubber cement, with both diagonal corners cut so it could be used on either side. We never even tried it because the rubber cement on the sides would not let our fingers go when we tried to pick one up.

There were also all sorts of Emery labels, and one guy had actually made a dimensioned blueprint with tolerances, and brought a set of micrometers to check what we had made. To make a long story short, we found that labels on the tape cut with scissors would work half the time. So we had ten pairs of scissors and a hundred labels every night, and used the HP65 as our quality inspector. Needless to say, we each had a copy of every program that we thought fit to write.

Since I had the 65 seven days a week, and everyone else only saw it Monday, Wednesday, and Friday nights for a couple of hours, a very large percentage of all the programs were mine. Since I was in grad school and most were under-grads, I was being asked a lot for instructions and listings and flowcharts, which I generated.

Well, the month that they gave me was up, so it was time to pack up copies of all the programs and send them off. When I got to more than a hundred, I began to tire of copying and making tapes, so I called and asked for help. So many people came over that they couldn't all work on the 65, so they started labeling the cards and drawing pictures on them and Scotch-taping card holders on the documentation pages. Then they started judging them as to whether they would buy the program if it were for sale. We finally mailed HP about a hundred of the two hundred and fifty we had, and thought that they would be impressed, and we waited for our much-deserved pat on the back.

It took three weeks, but I got a package in the mail of the Machine Design, the Stress Analysis, and the Chemical Engineering PACs with beautiful documentation and brand new cards in a carrying case. On the instruction book they had acknowledged me by name. WOW! My chest stuck out so far I couldn't see the ground. *On the same day*, the registered letter was delivered which said that we had violated HP's patent for making cards, and we should cease and desist from all further sales and would be sued for any profit that we had made to date. Boy, does that deflate a big chest.

I tried to call Dick Bauman and was told: "He doesn't work here any longer." That is the last time I have talked to anyone from APD.

I had to get a lawyer, and when I did, he found out that they had a *process* patent, and since our process was not theirs, they had no claim. Further, their statement that we had sold them was untrue, and therefore libel. So the whole thing was dropped like a hot potato.

They never asked for the prototype back, and I assumed that some day it would be the flagship of my collection of HP calculators. *Then*, in 1983, our house was robbed, and the prototype is somewhere out there, probably at a flea market. It has no serial number, and there is a lot of wear on it.

Twenty-five years later, I ran into Dick Bauman on an HP calculator chat room. Boy, was I wrong—I thought *we* had got him fired because of our cards. It turns out that some kid named Wozniak, who had worked for him during the summer, had offered him a job at a new start-up named 'Apple'. Back then, if you quit HP, you were walked to the door. His pride and joy still is the HP80 presented to him for being the program leader; he still uses it. He has to because his net worth isn't seven figures, it is eight.

Just when you thought it was over and going to settle down, THE BIG BANG—all at the same time:

- the HP65 was introduced

- the ALTAIR was introduced

- PPC started

- the Dayton HP65 uses group became DMA (Dayton Microcomputer Association)

- computer clubs and calculator clubs and newsletters like *Homebrew*, *Micro-8* and *Dr. Dobb's* were published and exchanged everywhere

- the DEC VAX was available to engineering departments (no more 360 from MIS that you could not use)

But that is the start of another subject.

Richard Nelson, founder of the original PPC, was kind enough to provide us with the following comments on the setting up and development of user groups. Some of his remarks are of historical value, others apply as much to new clubs today as they did twenty-eight years ago.

STARTING A CALCULATOR CLUB

RICHARD J. NELSON (1)

With HPCC's long history, it is appropriate that they examine and review some of the many events and accomplishments of their members.

There were many foreign chapters in the U.K., Germany, Italy, France, The Netherlands, Sweden, and Finland—only HPCC survives today. David Burch founded the club some twenty years ago, and I remember staying with him when we had the first conference at a London hotel. I don't remember a lot of the details, as we were all strangers getting together for the first time. It was fascinating to me to see other ways of living, from on-demand electric water heaters (not common in the US) to the international magazines David subscribed to. We Americans are language-challenged.

At the first conference, I gave a talk on the HP-41. This followed a talk where the HP-75 was presented as being faster and more powerful than the HP-41. I asked the HP-75 enthusiast if he could write a counting program that would run and keep count in the display. He did and I asked someone in the audience to call out "start" and we had a race between the two machines. When "stop" was called out the two machines were compared with the larger number being the winner. Of course the HP-75 would win, and the only question in the audience's minds was by how much. When the race was finished, the HP-41 had won. What a surprise... until I told everyone that I "cheated". My HP-41 program was written in machine code. Old-timers will remember what was required to accomplish this. Today, the HP48/49 machines mix machine code, System RPL and User RPL together in the same program.

The HP49 was "born" at the HPCC 15th Anniversary Conference in September 1997. This conference attracted top-notch programmers from France. Interviews for programmers took place "in the back room" as the conference was being conducted. The team that HP hired knocked all of our socks off with their Programming Contest entry in all three HP-48 languages. But these are recent events—I am getting ahead of the story.

During the early 1960s my primary hobby was amateur radio. I held an Advanced Class License and operated in the US as WA6OBM and in the Philippines (1964 -1968) as DU1DBT—Don Bosco Technical Institute—where I was the electronics department head. I was very active in amateur radio in both countries and I wrote the newsletter for the local amateur radio clubs. This was quite unusual in the Philippines because I was a foreign member of the Philippine Amateur Radio Association, PARA.

In the spring of 1972 I bought an HP-35. It was a very expensive purchase ($395 in 1972, $1,694 in 2002 US dollars) for a young family (wife & 3 young children) to make. Once I became familiar with the HP-35, my favorite pastime was writing down keystroke routines on 3 x 5 cards to most effectively solve problems. The idea was to minimize the number of keys to press in a loop by allowing "extra" keystrokes to set the loop up. I was working in electrical engineering and, until that time ,we did most of our calculations on the slide rule. The ability to have ten digits of accuracy was intoxicating.

When the HP-65 was announced two years later, I was ready for programmability. The price was really too high but I still went down to the local HP sales office and watched a video that presented the machine. I simply could not believe my eyes, all that power for *only* $795! ($2,891 in 2002 US dollars) I sold my model 28 Teletype machine along with some other gear and raised the $795 required to acquire the world's most powerful computer—this claim is based on memory, size, and weight. Soon my amateur radio interests faded as the calculator consumed all of my time. I searched for other users, but I couldn't find any. HP calculators were sold directly by HP sales people and I contacted "my" salesman to ask if he could give me the names of other customers. He said he would talk to a few of them to see if they would agree to let him give me their telephone numbers.

Xerox machines were in use in those days but they were very expensive, and I had a special account with my employer—Hi Tek in Santa Ana, California—to use their machine to produce the amateur radio newsletter. The mailing technique I used was to type the names and addresses on a long adding machine tape. I would fold and staple the newsletter and mail it with the outside cover back as the address label. Ron Johnson, editor, uses a similar technique with the CHIP newsletter. I would tape the newsletter cover sheet to the outside copy glass of the Xerox machine and slide the adding machine tape through two slits in the sheet. The cost for copies was cheaper in larger quantities, so I set the machine to do 100 copies at a time, and advanced the adding machine tape with each pass of the exposure lamp. I "personally" addressed each copy each month.

When I identified a few Orange County/Los Angeles area people who used the HP-65, I decided that I would write a newsletter dedicated to this machine. I called it 65 *Notes*, wrote up a few ideas on two sides of a single sheet, and the club was born in June 1974. This was an easy and natural thing to do since I had done amateur radio newsletters in two countries for a decade. Once I had a piece of paper for people to read, word began to spread. HP sales engineers could photocopy issue No. 1 and people could contact me; I soon had material for issue No. 2. At the same time, HP promised their own newsletter and we were wondering when it would get started. Calls to HP informed us that it was very soon—August was the month. Could I get out three issues before HP got their first issue out? I made it by a few days.

By this time, copies of the newsletter had reached HP, who were in Cupertino in northern California at that time—they moved to Corvallis later. After each of us had produced a few issues, it was a natural thing for the editors of the two "competing" newsletters to talk on the phone. I had changed companies by then and I worked for Statek, a maker of low-frequency quartz crystals for the then-new digital watches. Statek had signed a technology transfer agreement with Litronix, also in Cupertino. Litronix wanted to make watch crystals, in addition to non-scientific calculators, using our silicon wafer technology, and I was soon making trips north. I arranged a visit to HP and I met Henry Horn, HP's editor. We struck it off immediately and became very good friends. I even wrote articles for HP's newsletter. The ones I remember most are an early article on the HP-41 (complete with a young photo), and a follow-up article five years later. Henry even came to some of our meetings.

Starting a club dedicated to the technology that I felt passionate about consumed me for ten years. I was spending every spare hour of the day while working a full-time job. I split my day into two parts, eating when I got home from work, taking a 90-minute nap (1 sleep cycle), and then working until the early morning hours on the club. I was burning the candle at both ends and I had occasionally fallen asleep at traffic lights while driving home—thank goodness Włodek doesn't drive that much.

The ties with Henry rapidly developed, and I became a regular visitor to HP. We communicated freely, each respecting the others "territory" and each helping the other as needed. One of the blanks I had on the HP-65 User's Club membership form was for each new member to write down the serial number and date of purchase of their machine. From this data I could determine how many machines were being built; this created great difficulties at HP. They were super-sensitive of their sales numbers—this hasn't changed—and I was publishing them. Henry was called to a meeting to discuss this terrible thing, and he told them that they should not be upset with me when it was their fault. He told them that I could determine the number of machines built because of the format of the serial number. They changed their "serial number code" after that meeting.

The membership grew, and people across the country started "chapters". The first was in Dayton, Ohio organized by Dean Lampman—the story of Dean's contributions could fill a book. The *Lampman Split Logic*, the *Lampman correction factor*, and Dean's "over-the-top" interest in new technology made his chapter's activities world-famous in later years, because his chapter went on to found the largest personal computer club that is still very active today. The second chapter, CHIP, was organized by Jack Stout, which is also still active today. The CHIP chapter sponsored HHC 2001, and Dean drove in to attend. It was really great to see him after so many years—you can see his photographs on the HHC 2001 CD.

The HP-65 gave way to the HP-67, and the club name became a problem. By that time we were quite well known, and the search for a new name began. One of the acronyms frequently used in articles was PPC. I believe that someone (Jake?) researched the old issues and determined that Craig Pearce may have been the first to use it. When it became time to pick a new name, I thought that PPC would be good and the world-famous club that would have chapters in 63 countries was born. At the time, I had written down nearly fifty different meanings for PPC: *Pocket Programmable Calculator, Personal Programmables from Corvallis,* and *People Programming Computers* are a few. There were also non-calculator related uses of PPC, such as *Professional Photographers of California* that you could find in the telephone book. When the HP-41 replaced the HP-67, and we were near our peak of membership and activity, HP pressured us to incorporate. PPC then became the *Personal Programming Center,* and HP could better work with us by including the club brochure in each calculator box.

In late 1975, and certainly by January 1976, the HP-65 Users Club started publishing tips, routines, programs, and unsupported feature information on the TI SR-52 Scientific Programmable Calculator. By May of 1976 (*65 Notes,* V3N4P5) a decision was made regarding non-HP calculators. A Club Activity Policy was announced: "The HP-65 Users Club will restrict its activities to Hewlett-Packard personal programmable calculators".

At this time I also announced that regular column editor Richard C. Vanderbough would start the SR-52 Users Club based in Dayton, Ohio. The membership contribution was $6 for six months of the newsletter, *52-Notes,* with the first issue published in June 1976. Looking back, it seems strange to see TI and HP calculator programs being published side by side. Richard Vanderbough continued his *HP 55/25 Notes* column through the June issue. In July, Hal Brown took over the *HP 25 Notes* column and Bob Edelen took over the *55 Notes* column. At this time, Craig Pearce of the CHIP chapter started *The Micro Scene* column. I knew that personal computers were coming and I wanted this column to prepare our members for a computer newsletter—which it eventually did. Another surprising "fact" was the tremendous success that Hal Brown had with the *25 Notes* column. Most members simply didn't believe that Hal did not have an HP 25. The HP-25 material published over its lifetime is an amazing story in itself.

The May 1976 issue of *65 Notes* also contained a pre-announcement of the National 7100 calculator. In September, I announced that Dean Lampman (41) would start a club dedicated to the NS-7100: "The mechanics, goals, and even the first issue subject content have been blocked out. The rest is up to National." The new machine, the first to use non-volatile memory for writable program memory modules, never made it into production.

There was another club that was started to support Casio machines. This was started by a student in Utah, but I don't remember the details, and I don't think that it lasted very long, perhaps a few months.

All other clubs that I am aware of started as chapters of PPC. I actively encouraged the many people I talked to who wanted to start a club. Never once did I worry about "competition"—you will understand when you realize the requirements.

Many students used HP calculators in their studies. They loved the excitement of programmability and the tremendous advantage that they had with their class work. So many students called me, often referred to me by HP, to ask how to start a club that I wrote articles on the subject. I usually described the process and requirements of the founder. I cannot remember a single school club that was started by a student that lasted a calendar year.

One of the vital aspects that I tried to instill in these enthusiasts is one I learned in the Philippines when I was publishing the Philippine

Amateur Radio Associations newsletter. I produced many regular "packed" issues. Once I was asked by my wife about the work I did. She said: "you work so hard at doing this and 'they' don't appreciate it." Then I realized what it was about—I don't do it for 'them', I do it for me. This attitude or motivation is a vital value I tried to encourage in all club founders.

My advice to the students was to clearly understand their motives in starting and running a club. I pointed out that if they were seeking accolades and ego-stroking, that they would soon be disappointed. If they thought that such an activity would make them famous—within their own social or campus circles—they would be disappointed. I really emphasized that the work and organization of it all had to be fun for them or the club wouldn't survive. Thinking, observing, listening, planning, organizing and communicating is just plain hard, tedious work. For most human beings it is far easier to emote than to think.

What have I learned from starting a calculator club 10,339 days (28.3 years) ago? I believe that I learned a most vital lesson—remember that most technical people are not very socially conscious—from living in the East for six years during three visits over a ten-year period. The lesson, obvious to most normal people I suppose, is: People do extraordinary things for other people. Yes, people do things for God and Country on the macro scale, but on the day-to-day micro scale we all are willing to expend resources for our family and friends. I believe that this is fundamental to human nature, and a vital aspect of club operation.

As intelligent, thinking people, however, we also have a more ideal and noble side. We think of ideas that sound good but can't actually work in practice—or can they? I have written about this frequently over the years, especially in times of crises. Most of my HP club material is stored in a room 10' x 20' x 13' in Orange Country 85 miles south of where I live near Magic Mountain, north of Los Angeles, so I will have to provide an incomplete reckoning of these values and principles.

Here are the values I believe in, and have attempted to practice with the club:

1. **It is an open group.** There are no secrets. All activities are openly discussed. There are no hidden/management activities.
   Example: PPC under board management "died", CHHU lived.

2. **Sharing is a vital activity.** You are here to share what you know. Remember #1.
   Example: There was never a shortage of material to publish.

3. **Resources are distributed.** Each member brings and contributes resources. Remember #2.
   Example: The readers prepared indexes to the newsletters.

4. **Ideas are work.** If you have an idea, share it. If it is a good idea—known by a positive response from the group—you may work on it. If you need resources, remember #3.
   Example: Every meeting has a "show and tell".

5. **Recognize and respect (the work of) others.** Remember and credit the ideas and work of others in the club. Remember #4.
   Example: Lampman Split Logic, Phase 1 interrupt switch.

6. **Show, don't just tell.** We are an enthusiastic group who practices the concepts of technology. Don't just tell me, show me how. Remember #5.
   Example: Full page photos of machine internals.

7. **Focus on the goal.** If all of the above are practiced, you will contribute your resources because you believe in the club and the project at hand. Individual issues are more easily "given up" if the member understands and agrees to the goal.
   Example: PPC ROM - $238,000 (more than half a million in 2002 US dollars) donated and hundreds of people working for two years without a single penny of compensation.

What are my motives in maintaining an organization of people who have Hewlett-Packard calculators as their focus? Certainly, the unique qualities of HP's calculator products is one motive. I have tried to express this idea in many articles over the last 28 years. If, however, I look at what I personally get from all this, it is simple. No matter what meeting of people I have attended, and I have attended over 800 meetings, from Mexico, Sweden, the UK, to the US, I have noticed something very interesting. It didn't matter where I was because the people were all like-minded. They were technical people. They were very intelligent people. They were very curious, and they were all happy to be with people of similar interests.

Most importantly they shared similar values. They valued education and teaching.

What motivates me? I truly enjoy learning new technology and having fun with it. Curiosity got me started, learning and fellowship keeps me going, and writing about it makes it worthwhile.

Have I been successful with the club? I suppose that the answer will depend on your definition of success. Here are ten measures of success. If the measure is:

1. **Longevity**, the answer is unknown, we continue today after 28 years.

2. **Accomplishment**, the answer is yes. A book could be written about the accomplishments of our members, just as HPCC members are writing this book.

3. **Member education**, the answer is yes. We published proceedings for 25 conferences. We published 5,200 pages of newsletters not counting the work of the chapters, with 2,000 words to a page.

4. **Member advancement**, the answer is yes. Many, many members— some to this day—have told me that their careers and professional lives have been improved because of their club membership.

5. **Having fun**, the answer is an unchallenged yes. No examples needed—another book?

6. **Structured organization**, the answer is probably no.

7. **Contributing to the advancement of calculators**, the answer is yes—
    this could be a third book.

8. **Being remembered positively**, I have to say yes.

9. **Being efficient**, of course. How can you compare a person hired to
    solve a problem with a person who spends his or her spare time on a
    problem simply because it is fun?

10. **Recording our work**, Yes, Yes, Yes. Our publications, conferences,
    projects and meetings are recorded on film, paper, video, and CDs.
    All of our work is available to anyone who is interested. I will bet
    that club members have more information on HP calculators than
    HP does.

Yes to 9 out of 10. Is that good? What others should be added? Is
number 6 really required? I certainly never dreamed of the thousands of
HP users I was to meet when I first saw the HP-65 and was "blown
away". There are many things I never dreamed when I started a
calculator club. Perhaps that is the point.

X < > Y, and Happy Programming.

Richard J. Nelson

GROWING & CHANGING

Why was this an opportune time to set up a British club for HP calculator users? The HP-41 family of calculators, introduced in 1979, had become well-established among people who needed a personal computer. The IBM desktop personal computer had not yet been introduced. A variety of personal computers was already available, but these were expensive, and each had its own foibles. The HP-41 provided an affordable and portable alternative. In addition, a range of commands not described in the manuals had been discovered. There was a need for a means to spread information about the HP-41 and especially about Synthetic Programming. The Internet was not generally available, and clubs were an excellent way to share information—and they also provided a way to meet people with similar interests.

We were learning about how to run a club—and also how to get the best from our calculators, how to hack them by breaking into the system programming—and even how to hack the hardware. RabinEzra, one of our founder members, recalls those days.

THE EARLY YEARS

RABIN EZRA (19)

It is now difficult to remember that, at the beginning of HPCC's life, the choice of programmable calculator or desktop machine was much harder to make than it is now. The issue of PCW which carried a cover story on the Sinclair ZX80 also had a review of the HP-41C. To my 13-year-old eyes, they seemed in some sense similar in the possibilities they offered, with the latter having the advantage that I would be able to carry it around, and it would remember my programs when I turned it off. Today, the gulf in computational power between the laptop on which I type this, and the 48SX on the table, make their respective roles clear.

Somehow, I managed to convince my sceptical parents that they should buy one for me. As part of HP's support activities, it produced a newsletter called *HP Key Notes* containing programs and news. In Vol. 6 No. 2, a letter from David Burch announced the formation of PPC-GB. (Its name changed to PPC-UK by the actual start of the club.) Having already discovered the wonders of "Synthetics" thanks to the green Wickes book, I was keen to see what else people had discovered and so joined.

The first major event was the U.K. conference held at a remarkably grand location (or so it seemed to me, as a 15-year-old). Rather than using a college venue, the conference was organised at the Great Northern Hotel in Kings Cross in London. For me, it provided an opportunity to see hardware which had previously only been pictures in catalogues. The various peripherals were probably what made the 41 a computer system rather than a calculator, even if I couldn't afford them at that time.

The conference also saw the introduction of the HP-75C. I remember being stunned by the slide show of one in bits, as it hadn't occurred to me that someone might take such an expensive piece of equipment to pieces simply out of curiosity. It also saw a debate as to whether the 75C, perhaps the first ultra-light laptop computer, should be supported by the club. The consensus that eventually emerged was that we should support the HP aspects of the machine, but not print BASIC programs which might work on any machine.

Sadly, I missed out on perhaps the most important part of any conference; being rather younger than the other attendees I had not opted to stay at the hotel, but rather to commute. I therefore didn't stay for the late-night informal sessions, which I only discovered had happened when Vol. 1, No. 3 dropped on the mat. With issue 3, the journal gained a card cover and photos of the sessions, as well as the more normal part of the conference. I even managed to sneak into a picture, though nobody knew who I was, so the list of people under the picture labelled me "?".

The 41, and RPN machines in general, remained the main "FOCaL" point of the club across the first few years of its existence. Even with the 75 and HP-71B, there remained a feeling that the club's constituency was predominantly RPN machines. As well as conventional ways of programming them, the club also provided a forum for those of us interested in m-code programming.

It was in connection with this that the club attempted its first hardware project. As I had some electronics skills, I became involved. To write machine code for the 41, a box capable of simulating a plug-in ROM was required as the memory spaces used for user data and programs were physically distinct from that in which m-code executed. The 41's processor had a serial bus, so interfacing more conventional components to it required a set of shift registers and some assorted decode logic. As an additional oddity, the words were 10 bits wide, so some packing logic was required if space in conventional 8 bit memory parts was not to be wasted. Eventually the club chose to simply provide a service for members by sourcing ERAMCO units as a full design could not be justified.

The release of the HP-28C marked the close of the early years of HPCC. With its release, HP moved from expandable, interfaceable machines to much more targeted products. Though later products could take memory cards, they assumed that for I/O, the owner would have a PC to connect to. As well as being a closed box, the 28 marked a major change in the usage model; out went the type-limited four-level stack, and in came a completely polymorphic, infinitely deep one. The programming language also changed.

HPCC did pull a 28C apart to check on the feasibility of adding more memory, as it was based on the same processor as the 71B. One quiet evening at Imperial College, I took a drill to the heat sealed case to open it. The machine appeared, reassembled, on the following journal cover with the keys rearranged and still functioning, though lacking a little in the solidity "stakes".

(These days, the HP I use most is a 16C, without which I would be lost.)

Some of our founder members went to work with, or for, Zengrange. The name "Zengrange" sounded strange—perhaps a mix of Eastern mysticism and British homeliness. The story of Zengrange ran parallel to that of HPCC for over ten years.

ZENGRANGE & JOHN FRENCH

GRAEME CAWSEY (25)

Although calculators had been user-programmable for some years, it was the HP-41C that marked the advent of the truly customisable calculator. It had expansion slots. No longer the requirement to spend half an hour feeding it unreliable magnetic cards—your application could be stored on a ROM module. This, together

Calc-o-rama: HP-41s and HP-71s at Zengrange
Photo by Frank Wales

with features such as an alphanumeric display, made it an ideal handheld tool for industry. HP themselves produced a number of ROM modules for different industry sectors—surveying, petroleum, statistics etc., but the market was now open for companies to have bespoke applications written.

Zengrange Ltd was founded at the start of the 1980s by John French and Kit Hamar. John was a programmer who had previously developed an accounting package for the HP-41, and Kit was a designer. The company had beaten off competition from Marconi to build a handheld mortar fire computer for the British Army. MORZEN, as it was called, was based around the HP-41 with custom ROM modules, a rubber keyboard overlay and the famous 'Battlecase'—a fully customised calculator.

When I joined in 1982, the company had just started work on GUNZEN, the equivalent to MORZEN, but for the bigger toys that the Royal Artillery play with. Assembly level programming on the HP-41 was in its very infancy: HP Corvallis had supplied to us the source code listings of the internal ROMs and a map of the CPU registers and we had an EPROM box from Handheld Products in the U.S.. The rest we had to work out.

The working out was fun, if a little tortured. There were no assemblers or debuggers, everything was done by punching in three-digit strings of hexadecimal numbers. Mistakes couldn't be found until the code was run, and the method of correction was to re-burn the EPROM. After 20 years I still have those opcodes burned into my long term memory: 130: LDI, 3E0: RTN, etc..

Zengrange found HPCC to be a good source of young and enthusiastic HP-41 programmers: Frank Wales, Julian Perry, Ian 'Tarquin' Mitchell, Paul Vickers and yours truly amongst those calculator devotees who trod the path to Leeds. HPCC founder, and then editor, David Burch wrote our manuals for end-user products such as ZENROM and the ZEPROM Programmer.

After finishing the main development of GUNZEN, we were given time to work on ZENROM, a set of programming utilities for the user community; a sort of payback to the user club that had provided the company with its engineers. Working on ZENROM was a great experience: there were no predefined specifications to work to, it could include anything we wanted. The bits I remember most fondly were writing the DECODE function, and developing what we called "Direct-Key Synthetics". The DECODE function, which converted the X register to a hexadecimal string in ALPHA, was fun because there seemed to be an unofficial competition to write the shortest code to perform the action. As I recall, someone from the Finnish club had published the shortest at the time. After many hours cogitating, we managed to write one a single word shorter, but only by relying on a 'feature' of the CPU and how it handled the addition of hexadecimal digits whilst in decimal mode.

Unfortunately, even ZENROM had a deadline—the production of the masked-ROM had been booked with HP. With no time left, we were still three bytes over the maximum and could find no more code to shave.

(Ah, those were there days: when you really did count the bytes, not the megabytes!) In the end, we had to use the ROM version number and checksum bytes for code.

Colin Webb, Zengrange sales manager, and I travelled to Los Angeles to visit PPC and demonstrate ZENROM. PPC had recently undergone a 'change of management' and, after attending a meeting of the club, we were invited to dinner by the new management. They took us to a local restaurant in Orange County, and we were surprised to find the establishment empty save for our party. It transpired later on, that the restaurant wasn't empty due to unfavourable reviews or such like. Rather, we had gone to a Japanese restaurant on Pearl Harbor Day!

Zengrange continued to develop modules for GUNZEN, along with other HP-41-based military products such as ZENCRYPTER. The company expanded into electronics design, building its own ROM emulator, a development that eventually led to the ZEPROM module and accompanying programming software.

It was not the HP-41 that was used in Zengrange's biggest contract, it was the HP-71. The Department of Health and Social Security, as it was then, required a method to locate files as they moved around their offices. The resultant *Case Paper Location System* was based on HP-71s with Zenwand barcode readers, connected via HP-IL and linked to a network database. Six thousand HP-71s were used over 200 offices around the country. The system was the largest implementation of HP-IL ever attempted. It stretched the interface loop to its limits—and beyond.

The HP-71 was also used as a prototype for the In-Flight Sales Unit, a point-of-sale system for duty-free sales on board aircraft. However, the single-line display, amongst other limitations, meant the HP-71 was dropped in favour of a system designed and built in-house. This marked the end of Zengrange customising HP calculators for its products, future systems all used in-house electronics. (The one, final project involving HP calculators was the *HP-41 Emulator* for the HP-48.)

Although the company continued for a while after the 'calculator' years, the engineers who had designed and developed those systems left to pursue their careers elsewhere. Zengrange was a fun place—more like a toy factory than a place of work. This was mostly due to the management style of its founder, John French, who gave the engineers the freedom they needed to learn and develop. John could be infuriating too; he enjoyed a good argument, often adopting the most preposterous positions. But such debates were always good-natured. John lost control of Zengrange in 1989 and set up a new R&D based venture, Grep Ltd, employing a number of ex-Zengrange engineers.

John French
Photo by Frank Wales

Zengrange itself was split up a few years later: the military side was sold to another defence contractor, and continues to this day as Zengrange Defence Systems. The commercial side was sold to a management buy-out, and still operates under the name TrackIt Systems.

PPC-UK received a lot of help and support from dealers and companies. Particularly helpful was Tony Collinson, who provided calculator support at HP(UK). Members of PPC-UK would often run into other members at branches of the computer and calculator company Metyclean who gave us help—and discounts. The Metyclean shop opposite Westminster Cathedral in London was especially popular. RMS in Birmingham also gave PPC-UK members discounts—and continue to do so. The best-known dealer to provide support and sell esoteric bits of kit was EduCALC in California. Here, its founder, Jim Carter, describes how EduCALC was set up, and eventually closed down.

A SHORT HISTORY OF EduCALC

JIM B. CARTER

EduCALC was the by-product of a book, written by Dr. George McCarty, a Ph.D. mathematician from the University of California, called *Calculator Calculus,* and a calculator display used to teach students. In 1976, Interfab Corporation contracted with George McCarty to manufacture calculator displays using large 1½ inch digits that could be read from 60 feet away. Students could see the display in real time in the classroom, and thereby increased their attention span considerably. The digits were later turned around to be visible by the user from a few inches and enabled legally blind people to use calculators. George and I used the mailing list from *Calculator Calculus* to develop a customer base. We used the mail-order facility and personnel at Interfab to send out literature and process orders. Our mission was to keep prices low and technical content high. In a very short time, George and I were on our way.

The first catalog was a six-pager. As the catalog grew in page count, to 128, our distribution grew to most of the civilized world and well over a million copies a year. Four issues of the catalog were published each year to keep up with new products. The last catalog was published in 1997, #74, and had shrunk to sixty-four pages. We even printed a full-color catalog, #73.

The first few catalogs didn't even contain calculators, and were known as the 'EduCALC mail store'. We sold a lot of books about calculators, but customers wanted calculators as well, so in catalog #11 we sold our first HP-41C for $145 (List price $195). Olympic Sales was our competitor, but we were intent on being more technical with honest,

59

straightforward verbiage. The technical calculators were beginning to
have a real effect on our society, and HP was recognized as the top of
the line. Our mission was to educate the world about calculators.

We decided early on that HP would be
the best partner we could team up with,
and the HP reps had a genuine interest in
our success. Howard Brook, one of our
HP reps, used his influence to get us
established in the HP family, and TG
Neely coined the phrase: "show the
customer how a calculator will change his
life." This later became our mission
statement. We wanted every customer to
be glad he came to EduCALC; we even
had an official greeter, Kaycee, a large
Collie dog (WalMart perfected the idea).

We treated the HP factory in Corvallis,
Oregon, like a partner and they

Włodek outside EduCALC in 1997

reciprocated. They respected our point of view and valued our opinion.
About that time, I met Richard Nelson. Along with our HP sales rep,
Richard and I went to the California Polytechnic State University at
Pomona California where Richard gave a talk about the HP-41 to a
math class. I could see he was in his element—he offered lots of
information, and couldn't wait for the next question. It was clear to me
that we needed him on our staff in order to progress to the next level.
He accepted my offer in the spring of 1987 and we were on our way. At
that time we had 27 employees.

Co-operation from the factory grew. They solicited our help on
technical aspects as well as sales (not that they always took our advice).
Richard developed "Technical Notes", as did customers, and HP
realized that EduCALC was a great source for technical support. We
stocked hundreds of items to help people get more from their
machines. We frequently received checks payable to Hewlett-Packard—
the distinction between HP and EduCALC was growing small as we

became HP's largest calculator dealer. With the introduction of the palmtop, EduCALC was able to market it in the same way.

Customers wanted to do more and more with their machines, which gave rise to third-party products from small companies. These companies were frequently too small to get the attention of HP, so EduCALC assumed the role of HP in providing advice, help and marketing. Richard was put in charge of product development. Third-party products grew to several hundred. Later we accepted trade-ins and sold used calculators. This worked well due to the high quality of the HP machines.

The computer became the standard in the computing field, and HP got deeper into computers. Calculator profits at HP were diverted to the development of palmtops and computers. Calculator advertising and interest dwindled; sales slowed. HP development teams were more interested in computers than calculators, and HP customers were no longer just engineers.

When calculator and palmtop operations were transferred to Australia and Singapore, it became harder and harder to maintain a partner relationship with HP. HP seemed destined to go it alone without dealers, using the Internet to drive sales as they discovered that they had lost the school market. Shortages became more frequent, sales reps didn't know the difference between RPN and Algebraic, and sales began to drop. During the peak of the HP48SX, we sold as many as 1,000 machines in one day. The market was changing, and HP seemed to make mistake after mistake in their marketing plans. Rules became the order of the day and ideas took a back seat. The magic in the relationship between HP and EduCALC became a business relationship. In December of 1997, it became clear that the good old days would never return.

Our official greeter, Kaycee, a large Collie, disappeared from home the month after we closed EduCALC, never to return. Dr. George McCarty died two years after the close, and I am now in the Horse Products business in Southern California.

DEVELOPMENTS

The early days of the club were marked with a great deal of excitement—and also uncertainty about where we were going. Gradually, we worked out what to do and how. The fact that we are celebrating the club's 20th anniversary suggests that we made the right choices—and that we were lucky, too.

What a club is called, and the details of its constitution, rarely have much effect on what actually happens at meetings. Yet people get incredibly involved in names and constitutions, and these can be the source of much discord until a decision is finally reached. Indeed, is it really a club if it has no constitution? Of course, some clubs have a constitution that says only: "There shall be no constitution." But PPC-UK was made of sterner stuff.

Constitution and name

Włodek Mier-Jędrzejowicz (9)

Early on, PPC-UK had a simple constitution written by a few founding members. As the club grew, some members wanted a more formal constitution. A debate about the nature of the constitution followed: David Burch preferred that it should be a reminder to us of what we are doing, while Neville Joseph, who was Treasurer at the time, wanted it to be close to a legal document. We eventually settled on a somewhat legal document while retaining a statement of what the club is. Some matters are not dealt with at all; Neville Joseph pointed out that these would be dealt with by Common Law if not covered in our constitution. This is now printed in the club's Member Pack every year; we shall not reprint it here. Changes to it have been limited in the past twelve years, which suggests that what was agreed then was close to what we need.

The constitution specifies that among the club's activities are to: "hold conferences and meetings," and "publish a journal, newsletter and other limited edition publications." As this book shows, the club has certainly done all that, and continues to do so.

The constitution states that: "The Club shall be known as the Handheld and Portable Computer Club," and that: "The Club's name shall be represented by HPCC." When the club was set up, it was the British chapter of PPC, and was called PPC-UK. This continued until the unfortunate split between Richard Nelson, founder of PPC, and the PPC Board. The PPC Treasurer at the time proposed that it be stated clearly that the PPC Board makes no claim on the assets of any Chapters, and the Board accepted that. Nevertheless, PPC-UK felt that it would be safer to make our independence clear, and to change our name. The PPC-UK committee wanted to keep a name similar to PPC, but also relating to HP. The letters HPCC fitted both requirements, but HP had previously objected to a club using 'Hewlett Packard' in its name, so HPCC officially stood for 'Handheld and Portable Computer Club', though it is no coincidence that it can also be read as 'HP Calculator Club'.

One possibly surprising omission is that the constitution does not say what should happen if the club were to shut down. There seemed to be no need for that to be considered when the constitution was written, and now the club committee avoids discussing the subject, for fear that even mentioning it might suggest to members that the club really is about to close. There are no plans to shut the club—we hope that it will continue for another 20 years—but at some stage, a section on closing the club will be added to the constitution, and may well be the source of a new sharp debate.

Other clubs grew and developed in different ways from HPCC. *The "Chicago Program Exchange", or* CHIP, *is one of the clubs that continue to prosper. Ron Johnson explains how.*

CHIP CHAPTER RECOLLECTIONS

RON JOHNSON

The Early Years

Craig Pearce, sometimes known as "pinball wizard", was the founder/
organizer of the CHIP Chapter in the fall of 1976. (That makes CHIP
twenty-six (26) years young!) I first met Craig at the calculator
counter on the first floor of Marshall Field's on State Street. That led
to my joining CHIP and then PPC. When Jack Stout was in hospital, he
read a magazine that mentioned the PPC group. That led Jack to join
PPC and then the CHIP Chapter.

After the "demise" of PPC, CHIP was a chapter of CHHU. In 1988, CHIP
became a chapter of HPX, the organization started by Brian Walsh.

Members

For many years, we assigned CHIP membership numbers. Being a chapter
of PPC, Richard Nelson was naturally given CHIP member #1. Craig
Pearce, as the organizer and coordinator, was #2. Members with very
low CHIP numbers who are still active include Randy Snively, Al Duba,
Bill Pryor, Jack Stout and Ron Johnson.

Craig Pearce resigned when personal computers became more
interesting than HP calculators. Jack Stout has been the Chapter Coordinator ever since.

Meetings / Meeting Places

Our first meeting place was the Stevens Restaurant in the Illinois
Center complex where Craig Pearce had some influence, or "clout" as
we say in Chicago. We met at classrooms at the University of Illinois

when Gary Lizalek was a student there. We met at the Byte Shop in LaGrange, the Data Domain in Schaumburg, a Denny's Restaurant, and mostly at Ace Metal Crafts where Jack Stout worked.

We've been meeting twice a month—on the first and third Wednesdays —for many years. Sometimes we have formal presentations, but often it's a "regular meeting"; essentially a social get-together. Paul Kettler has prepared many presentations on a variety of topics, such as: the probability of months with five Wednesdays; paper sizes; and the physics of a can-crusher.

Conferences / HP participation

Over the years, CHIP has hosted several full conferences, the latest being HHC2001. A couple of these conferences were held at HP's offices in a Chicago suburb. In addition, there were several "mini-conferences" held at Ace Metal. One of the more memorable times was in 1980, when we wrote a program on the HP-85 to generate HP-41 barcode—in Wes Staple's mobile home parked on Jack Stout's driveway.

On occasion, HP employees such as Bill Wickes and Eric Vogel have joined us, and told us what they could about HP's plans. Charles Lim from ACO met with us when in Chicago for a math teacher's conference in 1997. Several of us met with ACO people in April 2000, the day before they gave a sneak preview of the Xpander at NCTM 2000. But they wouldn't tell us anything about it.

Picnics / Parties

Starting in 1984 and running through 1994, Paul and Brenda Hubbert hosted eleven picnics at their home along the Fox River in Johnsburg (or McHenry) Illinois, northwest of Chicago. The picnics were usually held in early June, when the Consumer Electronics Show was in Chicago. The picnic was potluck style. Paul provided bumpy boat rides on the river. Jack Stout showed us how to play horseshoes in a vacant lot across the street. Calculators were not permitted at the picnics. In 1995, there was to be a picnic at a park, but very hot weather prompted a cancellation.

We've had several Christmas parties at the Maywood Park Racetrack. The first year we had a race named for the CHIP Chapter, and had the opportunity to ride in the pace car.

Activities

In the heyday of the 67/97 and the 41C calculators, the members of the group were quite active in programming and sharing tips. While most members bought the 48SX, the number of members actively doing programs for the 48 was rather small. Several 49G machines were purchased, but that machine was not well liked.

The current focus of the group seems to be discussing new toys of various flavors: PDAs, digital cameras, video camcorders, color printers, digital television, and so forth.

Newsletters

While there are some member letters going back to at least 1987, I've been writing the more formal CHIP Chapter Newsletter since 1991, usually with six issues per year. I'm still using a DOS-based word processor, printing to a Postscript printer, or to a Postscript file for "Distilling" to a compact Acrobat PDF file. All of these newsletters are available on the HHC2001 CD in one convenient PDF file compiled by Jake Schwartz. I find it quite interesting to go back through the old issues to see what was happening.

The Philadelphia area club was another successful chapter of PPC. *Jake Schwartz, who took part in its founding, recalls how it happened.*

Founding the Philadelphia-Area PPC Chapter

Jake Schwartz (878)

My history with Hewlett-Packard calculators began in 1971 when, as a Drexel University college co-op student working at the local RCA facility, I saw the HP9810 desktop programmable calculator for the first time. This was the first scientific machine which appeared at the plant that, instead of having fixed functionality and a large nixie-tube display, contained plug-in ROM cartridges, was programmable and used much more readable light-emitting diodes. The following year, the HP35 was announced and my dad and I ordered a unit together. We waited twenty-six weeks until the calculator was delivered, but it was certainly worth the wait. That year, my next co-op term took me back to RCA, but this time I got a significant amount of time working with, and programming, the older HP9100B desktop machine with its printer and mass memory and plotter peripherals.

Flash forward a few years to 1974 when the HP65 was announced. I was really tempted to plunk down the 800 dollars, but it just was too much for an undergraduate college student. The next year, the HP25 came out and I jumped at the chance to obtain my own programmable machine for less than $200. Following graduation, faced with the dilemma of either purchasing my own car or the HP65, practicality won out and I bought the car instead. So, I survived until 1976 with the HP25 until the HP67 at a "mere" $450 was announced, and I grabbed one as soon as it became available.

By this time, I was working as a bioengineer at the Children's Hospital of Philadelphia while pursuing a Master's Degree at nearby Drexel part time. The hospital was located just down the road on the adjacent

73

campus of the University of Pennsylvania, which had a wonderful college bookstore with a calculator store inside. They specialized in both HP and TI models, prominently displaying the top-of-the-line machines. Being the geek that I am, I tended to stop by the calculator counter frequently on my lunch hours. It was there in late 1976 when I met John Barnes (PPC #1067), a post-doctoral biochemistry student at University of Penn. John told me about the HP65 Users Club, and I quickly plunked down my membership fee, became member number 1820, and began receiving the *PPC Journal* in January of 1977. Ordering the back issues back to 1974 would soon follow, and I was overwhelmed with the amount of information available from like-minded people all over the country and the world.

It wasn't too long before I made my first call to the PPC clubhouse and had a nice conversation with Richard Nelson. I feel as if we hit if off fairly quickly, and had several additional conversations over the following months. Richard was working full time for Statek Corporation in Orange County, California at the time, and attempting to keep a fast-growing club afloat in his 'after hours'. Meanwhile, a few of the early PPC chapters were formed by Dean Lampman in Dayton, Ohio and by Craig Pearce in Chicago, Illlinois. Others were springing up rapidly.

Some time early in 1978, Richard mentioned in one of the PPC club phone bulletins that he would be making a business trip for Statek to the east coast of the U.S., and wished to meet with as many club members and chapters as possible. When John Barnes and I discussed this trip, John suggested that perhaps we should attempt to get as many members in the local Philadelphia area together to arrange to meet with Richard. This would also serve as a kick-off meeting for the formation of a Philadelphia-area PPC chapter. So, using the early PPC Member Handbook, which had a list of members sorted by location, we discovered that roughly 40 to 70 people lived in the vicinity. I contacted Richard to confirm our plans and pick a meeting date. A lecture hall at Drexel was available on that day, so we reserved it and then created a postcard announcing our intentions. John and I each paid for, and mailed, half of the cards.

A few days prior to Richard's departure, his business trip was canceled. I quickly suggested to John that we send a second postcard, announcing that, despite Richard's absence, we felt it would be a good idea for everyone to meet. I simply wanted to avoid the embarrassment of having to explain the situation to people after they made the special trip under false pretenses. John didn't feel that a second card was necessary, but I disagreed and sent a card to "my" half of the local member list.

So, on a weekday evening in May of 1978, John and I arrived early to Drexel with a few cases of cans of soda and buckets of ice and waited for people to arrive, not knowing what to expect. Much to our surprise, over 25 people showed up. We had to explain the "Richard situation" to some of them, and it seemed that everyone pretty much took the bad news well. It was a lively evening, with people showing off their HP machines and the various mods they made, such as HP67 speedup switches. There really wasn't a rigid agenda that night, but I believe everyone enjoyed it. We collected names and addresses, and agreed to meet again in three months. So, in August of 1978, the Philadelphia-area PPC chapter was officially born.

We met quarterly, alternating between Drexel University and the University of Pennsylvania, until the announcement of the HP41C in July of 1979, when we held a special meeting in the auditorium of the Children's Hospital of Philadelphia (where I was still working). The local dealer from the Penn bookstore was there with calculators, card readers and printers to sell, and ended up moving thousands of dollars of equipment that night. From that point, we agreed to meet monthly to discuss our newly-found excitement. (This coincided with Richard Nelson's California group increasing their meetings from monthly to weekly.)

The chapter had some high points over the nearly two-and-a-half decades to follow, not the least of which was our sending groups to both the 1980 and 1981 HP Handheld Conferences in Chicago and Corvallis, respectively. In Chicago, John Barnes gave a presentation announcing his book, *Pocket Programmable Calculators in Biochemistry*, which I was honored to review and help check the programs contained within for both the HP41 and TI58/59. (This was also the meeting where Bill Wickes first spoke in front of a large group on HP41C Synthetic Programming, and made initial contact with HP's Dave Conklin, which eventually got Bill hired there.) In Corvallis, we got to meet with more of the HP development team, and also experienced that unique moment when Jim DeArras of Richmond, Virginia (and the Washington D.C. chapter) discussed his unraveling of the HP41 machine-code instruction set with HP's Bill Egbert during the panel discussion. It was indeed an exciting time.

Perhaps the chapter's pinnacle was our hard work in 1980 to 1981 to compile, edit and document the PPC ROM Peripheral Routines. I will always remember that time, when we made frequent phone calls all over the country, sent and received numerous pieces of mail, held special evening and weekend chapter meetings for debugging sessions and hand-generated over 60 pages of the 500-page PPC ROM manual. It was indeed an honor to have participated in one of the most unique software projects anyone can remember.

Over the following ten years, chapter activity waxed and waned through the life of the HP41, 75 and 71B. After the demise of PPC in 1987, we renamed ourselves the Philadelphia-Area HP Handheld Club (PAHHC). With the introduction of the HP28C, some activity perked up, but in general it was difficult for the "traditionalists" to get used to this new-fangled RPL language. Not until the HP48SX was introduced, in March of 1990, did the group activity experience resurgence. Bill Wickes made a special visit to Philadelphia in November of 1990 to explain the HP48 and over 30 people attended. In the Spring of 1991, long-time HP Corvallis development team member Eric Vogel visited Philly to show us the HP95LX and the HP32S-II for the first time. This higher level of interest lasted through to the middle of the decade with the HP48GX and, to a lesser extent, the HP palmtops through to the HP200LX.

After 1995, HP development was in Singapore and the new team not only placed calculators on the back burner, but centered palmtop development around Microsoft's Windows CE operating system. This did not bode well for our group as far as maintaining interest was concerned, and monthly meeting attendance slowly dwindled. We did enjoy a second visit from Eric Vogel to show us the HP Logic Dart for the first time, plus enjoyed Włodek Mier-Jędrzejowicz's visit during one of his late-1990s U.S. trips. With the Australian Calculator Operation in 1998 and the '99 release of the HP49G, some additional interest was seen, but not nearly to the extent as with the HP48.

Lately, our gatherings have averaged three to four people, and unless something spectacular happens soon, I fear that it will only be logical to fold up the tent after our quarter-century run. Nevertheless, there have been no regrets along the way. I know my personal interest in handhelds will probably not wane and, hopefully, the new 2002 HP team will do something radical and really grab our attention.

COMMUNICATING

How do club members communicate among themselves? Meetings, conferences, club journals, letters to members, and telephone calls—many telephone calls—were the norm when the clubs were founded. It was not until the late 1980s that most clubs began to use email and the Internet as a serious tool. Since then, most clubs have been replaced by direct communications; others have learned to use the Internet as a means of communication.

One of the strengths of HPCC has been its club journal, Datafile. *As Jordi Hidalgo points out in his article later, this is what keeps contact between members who can not come to regular club meetings. The history of* Datafile *is intricately woven into the history of HPCC. Some clubs that used to publish a journal have moved entirely to electronic publishing on the web, but a printed magazine is still a better way to hold our club together.*

Datafile

Włodek Mier-Jędrzejowicz (9)

When David Burch started the club, he at once began work on a club journal too. This was unusual for a club, though some European clubs had their own journals too, since not all their members could read English. For its first two issues, the journal did not even have a name. After a lot of discussion and suggestions, the name *Datafile* was agreed upon.

David Burch continued to edit *Datafile* until the end of Volume 4. At that stage, no-one else was willing to become Editor, so *Datafile* was produced by an Editorial Committee who met at Imperial College and assembled available material into complete issues. The members of this Editorial Committee were: E. Browning, J. Cole, M. Cracknell, R. Ezra, and yours truly, W. Mier-Jędrzejowicz. Mark Cracknell agreed to take over as Editor with Volume 5, number 5, but the Editorial Committee continued to meet. *Datafile* continued to be produced by real "cut and paste"—articles were typed, and then cut out and pasted onto blank pages which were the masters sent to the printer. A lot of the articles were written by Mark Cracknell and me on our HP-75 computers, and were then printed on HP Thinkjet printers, then cut and pasted. Eventually the club purchased an IBM PC clone for Mark and there was less need for an Editorial Committee to help him.

Mark edited *Datafile* for 6 years, ably assisted by his mother, until Volume 11, number 6. Just after this issue had gone to the printer, he died in a car crash. I completed work on the last issue of Volume 11, issue V11N7/8, then Les Finch took over as Editor, beginning with V12N1. Les also took over the *Datafile* computer and made the editing job even more computerised, though some cutting and pasting continued.

Like previous Editors, Les had trouble getting enough material to fill
Datafile—the cover of V13N1 carried a wonderful cartoon of the HPCC
post room, with lots of mail for the Chairman, Secretary, and others,
but none for the Editor. Like other Editors too, Les worked wonders in
getting together enough material to continue producing *Datafile*, though
at six issues a year instead of eight, a change that had already been
arranged by Mark. A large proportion of the contents came from a few
prolific authors. In the early days, Frank Wales was one of these; later, I
began to write regularly. I must have written over 200 items by now.
Other authors frequently seen included Ron Cook, who was particularly
enthusiastic about mathematical questions, and Bill Butler, who has
been a constant source of fascinating insights into the HP48 family of
calculators.

As the Editors changed, so did the content of *Datafile*. From a magazine
full of articles about the HP-41, it gradually diversified to other HP
handheld calculators and computers, as these were released. Even now,
twenty years on, *Datafile* still sometimes has articles about the HP-41,
but the newer calculators, and articles of more general interest, take up
most of the space these days. An increasing amount of space is
dedicated to older models too. Articles about hardware are few and far
between, but thanks to a few dedicated enthusiasts, especially Tony
Duell, such articles continue to appear. It is to be regretted that so few
articles about the HP PDAs are submitted to *Datafile*. This may be
because they use a widely known operating system, Windows CE, so
users can read about it in many places, and do not need a specialist
journal such as *Datafile*.

Les edited *Datafile* for two years, but then he moved away from the
London area, and Roger Wiley took over with V14N5. Roger in turn
had to move home, and another period of editing by an Editorial
Committee began with V16N2. As Chairman, I found myself also
heading the Editorial Committee, for almost three years. Our most
recent Editor, Bruce Horrocks, took over with the V19N6, and I wish
him a long and successful Editorship.

The layout has changed too. Originally, *Datafile* was a set of photocopied A3 sheets, folded in the middle to give an A4 magazine. Then card covers were added, though on one memorable occasion the printers used extra thin paper instead of card. At the beginning of 1988, V7N1, the size was reduced from A4 to B5, to reduce the cost of posting the journal. The new size was not a success, and at the same time the printer began to produce very faint print on some pages. This was sorted out, but the size was unpopular and at the beginning of 1991 V10N1 moved to A5 size. Master copy was produced in A4, and was reduced to A5 by the printer. A5 is a standard size, for which containers and folders are more easily found, and *Datafile* has remained that size for the past eleven years. One innovation tried in a few issues more recently is the use of colour; a few issues have been published with colour photographs. This has been popular, but is very expensive, so few issues appear with colour now.

Datafile has been registered with an ISSN number, and a complete set has been lodged with the British Library. All issues from V1N1 to V20N6 have been scanned onto a single CD-ROM in time for HPCC's 20th anniversary conference, together with this book. The CD-ROM provides a compact source of old issues, but anyone who wants to write notes in a margin will still need the paper copies—or will have to print copies from the CD-ROM.

Mark Cracknell was Editor of Datafile *for longer than anyone else. He might well still have been Editor had he not died in a car crash. The following is mostly taken from his obituary in* Datafile *V11N7/8.*

MARK CRACKNELL

WŁODEK MIER-JĘDRZEJOWICZ (9)

Mark Cracknell, *Datafile* Editor from 1986 to 1992, was killed in a car crash on November 18th 1992. He was driving to work, in bad weather, early in the morning while it was still dark, and ran at full speed into an articulated lorry that was trying to do a U-turn, blocking the road. Those of us who knew Mark's driving were aware how careful he was—all the more reason for our sadness that this should have happened to him. The lorry driver was prosecuted and lost his licence, a small consolation to Mark's friends and family.

Mark Cracknell reading competition results at the 1992 HPCC Conference

Mark was born in India in 1951, the son of an ex-Army engineer who stayed in India after independence. As a child, Mark therefore saw how everything was made and done on the spot. As his brother Peter said, naturally he became an engineer. They grew up with their sister in a large ex-colonial house which their mother had inherited, then Mark went to boarding school in Blackpool and then studied Civil Engineering at Nottingham and Manchester universities. He graduated despite flooding a building with water from an experiment he was running—one of the stories he loved to tell at HPCC meetings. After graduation, he worked on overseas projects in Nigeria, Abu Dhabi and Oman, and he would tell stories from all these places. At first, he used a TI calculator on site, but eventually he threw it into a river and bought an HP on his next visit to Britain. He first came to one of our meetings in 1983, but then returned abroad, and communicated with HPCC by post. On his return to Britain, he went to Scotland, then came to Leighton Buzzard and became a regular at HPCC's London meetings. He joined the Committee, became *Datafile* editor, and set up a PC at home, to publish *Datafile*. This was the centrepiece of the room he called *Datafile's* "Mission Control", referring to himself as Editor Sahib. His Mother helped him with *Datafile* at times, and welcomed friends from HPCC who would sometimes visit to discuss *Datafile* matters, or to pack *Datafiles* into envelopes for sending to members. After Mark's death, HPCC continued to send *Datafile* to Mrs Cracknell and stayed in contact with her, largely thanks to Roger and Pauline Wiley.

There is not room here for more of Mark's stories, but maybe a separate book of them could be published.

The comp.sys.handhelds discussion group on Usenet was probably the first Internet tool that enthusiasts of HP handhelds used to exchange information and ideas. Then came bulletin boards and chat rooms. Nick Reid set up a bulletin board for HPCC in 1988, then Limitless provided us with a web home at www.hpcc.org which has provided us with service for nearly a third of the club's 20 years.

HPCC.ORG

THE WEB AS AN INFORMATION RESOURCE

MARK POWER (251)

The Internet has moved on a long way during the lifetime of HPCC.
Back when HPCC was formed, the Internet was for the military and the
occasional university. If you wanted to talk to a computer network, you
had to get hold of a hideously expensive green-screen terminal, a
ridiculously expensive acoustic coupler, and dial up a mainframe. Back
in those days, we relied on club meetings and *Datafile*. HP calculators like
the HP41 offered better networking capabilities than most computers,
but you had to have deep pockets to put together an HP-IL network of
more than a few devices, and you could only communicate with people
directly connected to your network.

In the late 1980s, bulletin boards started cropping up, allowing
computer hobbyists to communicate over greater distances. HPCC
members could dial in to *The No Zone*, where they could converse with
other like-minded people. HP's calculator division had its own bulletin
board where end-users could chat with the designers of their machines
—even if they were occasionally met with the HP 'blank stare'.

I used *The No Zone* and even tried the HP bulletin board directly. The
trouble was, the technology used by the calculators of the day and that
used to get on to the bulletin board were a bit tricky to interface to
each other. I often ended up printing out listings and then typing them
into the calculator. If you knew what you were doing, you could get
Kermit to transfer files to your machine. To get this to work reliably, I
ended up writing a terminal emulator program that ran on the HP48. At
the appropriate point, you could exit the terminal emulator and start a
transfer. This was all pretty hard work, and expensive.

Then, we started to get the backbone of the Internet as we know it today. Usenet news and e-mail became more generally available. At first, only people with networked Unix systems could get comp.sys.hp48. Later, everyone had access as news readers were ported to other platforms. Then Personal Computers started replacing workstations as a means of accessing the net, and prices dropped to a level where you could afford to connect up at home.

Nowadays, we take all this for granted. We have access to the world-wide web and e-mail on phones, PDAs, laptops, televisions, cameras and even microwave ovens and fridges.

People can now connect into comp.sys.hp48 and lurk, reading the chat of more gregarious people. The brave can enter discussions. If you want software, www.hpcalc.org has virtually every piece of software ever written for the HP48 and HP49, and quite a lot for the HP28. The HP41 is having a bit of a virtual renaissance at www.hp41.org. We even have a virtual HP calculator museum at www.hpmuseum.org where you can see pictures and read about older machines.

Numerous other sites provide interesting diversions for the dedicated. Gene Wright has a site with programs for virtually every programmable calculator from the HP-25 to the HP42S. On another site there is an HP-12C program for converting Maya dates to Christian dates.

If you have a Jornada, the Internet is directly accessible. The inclusion of a full web browser and e-mail tool in the latest generation of machines means you no longer need a PC in order to access vast amounts of software and online information.

The Internet has become a very useful tool for our club, allowing access to enormous quantities of information that were previously difficult to obtain. While HPCC has enthusiastic members, and until virtual meetings are as realistic as real life, and the Internet is as easy to read as *Datafile*, HPCC will survive. If you do want to go down the Internet route, just start at www.hpcc.org!

While Datafile *and the club's web site provide communication between all members, it is the meetings and conferences that provide the best form of contact. We have collected a few photographs to go with this article.*

CONFERENCES & MEETINGS

WŁODEK MIER-JĘDRZEJOWICZ (9)

HPCC activities began with the letters David Burch sent to people who contacted him, but things really got going with the first few meetings, as he mentions in his interview.

This shows a scene from the very first meeting, hosted by Graeme Cawsey in Lechlade. These first few meetings were soon followed by the club's first conference, again referred to by David in his interview.

The very first HPCC meeting

Whereas most of HPCC's meetings are ordinary ones, conferences have a special place in HPCC activities. They provide an excuse for members who do not come to ordinary meetings to come to a special one, and allow members to meet visitors from HP and from other clubs. HPCC's first major meeting was its conference in October 1982, and in 2002 the club celebrated its 20th anniversary with yet another conference.

In between, there have been conferences or mini-conferences almost every year. We have included here a few photographs from some of those conferences.

Recurring items at early conferences were the cakes, in the shape of a calculator, baked by Simon Bradshaw's mother. Here, we see Richard Nelson cutting one such 'calculator'.

Richard Nelson cutting the calculator cake

HP(UK) took our first conference seriously—John Golding, who was Deputy Manager at HP(UK). spoke to us about calculators and how we enthusiasts were "far out in the leading tail" of the distribution of users.

John Golding, Deputy Manager at HP(UK) speaking at the first HPCC conference in 1982
Photo by Włodek Mier-Jędrzejowicz

The conference was held in the Great Northern Hotel next to King's Cross station in London, an ideal place for people coming to London by train.

This photograph shows Richard Nelson (left) with Julian Perry (centre, with a Rubik's Cube; Julian wrote an HP-41 program that could solve the puzzle) and another attendee at the conference.

Julian Perry (centre) at the first HPCC conference
Photo by Włodek Mier-Jędrzejowicz

Richard spoke at the conference; David Burch is at the left.

David Burch (left) looks on as Richard Nelson speaks at the first HPCC conference in 1982

Photo by Włodek Mier-Jędrzejowicz

Here, Frank Wales is speaking about synthetic programming on the HP-41, with David Mulhall listening.

Frank Wales (left) speaking at the first HPCC conference while David Mulhall listens

Photo by Włodek Mier-Jędrzejowicz

There was no conference in 1983. Instead, PPC-UK participated in an HP show. The photograph shows George Ioannou (left) with a potential member.

George Ioannou (left) representing PPC-UK at an HP show in 1983

Photo by Włodek Mier-Jędrzejowicz

David Burch organised two more conferences in 1984 and 1985, at Chelsea College.

The photograph here shows Graeme Cawsey and Julian Perry (in his ZENROM t-shirt) at one of these conferences.

Graeme Cawsey and Julian Perry from Zengrange
Photo by Frank Wales

Here, Graeme is speaking at the same conference.

Since these early conferences, HPCC has held a major conference every five years, beginning with 1987, and one-day mini-conferences in the years between. Ordinary meetings have been the mainstay of club activity, though. The

Graeme Cawsey speaking at an HPPC conference
Photo by Frank Wales

early meetings were each organised separately, but soon a set of regular meetings was set up. Meetings were held in Leeds, Bradford, and Southampton, as well as Imperial College in London. The regular meeting site in London, at Imperial College, has now been in use for 19 years, and members and guests from all over the country and the world know that they can come to a meeting on the second Saturday of every month. The only exception is when the second Saturday falls on an Easter Saturday and the college is closed; then the meeting is moved to the third Saturday.

Special meetings include the Annual General Meeting every year, and one-off meetings. Some of these one-off meetings occur when there is a chance to meet a special guest: we have held such meetings at airports, and one in Bristol near the HP plant there when Bill Wickes was visiting. One particularly unusual meeting was an HPCC meeting held in Corvallis (where HP designed and built their calculators), when HPCC members invited everyone at an HP handhelds conference there to an English-style pub in the town.

Meetings provide the best chance for members to discuss programs, problems, and prognostications, to think of subjects for *Datafile* articles, and to join the work of the club Committee. Even if other HPCC activities were to wither, the club will continue so long as the regular meetings can continue.

The success of a conference depends on the help and co-operation of several people. One of our members, Gerry Rice, provided vital support at the 1997 conference—he provided the food and the barbecue. He is remembered for this, but more so for his programming and his stories.

GERRY RICE

WŁODEK MIER-JĘDRZEJOWICZ (9)

Gerry Rice was known in the club for his brilliant programming insights, and for his tales from the workfront—in Australia and in British business—as well as for his biting wit. His death was a sad loss to us all, but especially to a few friends who had come to look forward to his stories at each meeting in London. He was good at coining words and phrases: his description of the Australian outback, where he worked for a time, as the GAFA (Great Australian F... All) is particularly memorable.

Gerry was especially helpful on occasions that needed some work to be done. Despite being one of the older members of HPCC, he would always join in. He provided tea and coffee at HPCC's mini-conferences—and a barbecue at the 1997 conference! Gerry's acerbic wit came to the forefront on this occasion when he described the way he had been left to do all the work himself, while younger attendees stood around and watched him struggling to move the barbecue and cook on it. The barbecue was a great success; the 1997 conference and Gerry will be remembered for it.

His collection of calculators covered the Voyager models as well as the newer HP48 series, but he was most fond of the HP-41 and published programs for it in *Datafile* for some years. Even in hospital, he took along his HP-41, and went back to programming it as he got better. But he never recovered fully, and on his death left his calculators to be passed on to deserving members of HPCC. He continues to be remembered, and HPCC remain in touch with his family.

We have already commented on the importance of Datafile *as a means of communication with members unable to come to meetings. Jordi Hidalgo emphasises this point.*

Why we need Datafile

Jordi Hidalgo (1046)

Being an overseas member, I cannot enjoy anything greater than receiving *Datafile* every other month. The fact that it relies on members' contributions is what I like most, because it means excellent random articles most of the time. It is each author who decides how technical, useful, hilarious or amusing the articles will be.

When I joined HPCC three years ago (partly because there was no active students club in Barcelona) and the first issues arrived, I thought of submitting my own articles about tricks and small discoveries, but somehow the Internet was deemed to be more appropriate.

Until our Editor took a couple of my writings from a Usenet newsgroup, I did not realize that *Datafile* is the most suitable place for them, provided that someone can help remove my numerous grammos … many thanks, Bruce!

DESIGN

HPCC and the other HP handhelds user clubs were successful because they supported the use of products that aroused interest, and pride. We asked a few members of HP's design teams for their thoughts on the calculators that they worked on.

Bill Wickes was first an HP calculator user, then an enthusiastic PPC member, and then took a job at HP and became team leader for the HP-28C, HP-28S and HP48SX calculators, which all used a new version of the RPN interface. He explains here his thoughts on RPN.

A REALLY PATHETIC NAME

REFLECTIONS ON THE RPN WARS

BILL WICKES (696)

Reverse Polish Notation a.k.a. RPN. Was there ever a worse choice of name for a user interface, more sure to scare customers away? Sometimes I long for the good old days when engineers ruled the roost at HP, but in this case at least the next-bench guys would have done well to defer to their marketing colleagues and come up with a less intimidating name. The "algebraic operating system" phrase used by TI for their calculators isn't much more illuminating, but somehow it has always been more palatable to potential customers.

Common mathematic notation has several different ways to combine functions with their arguments—sometimes functions are written between their arguments, sometimes before, sometimes not at all, e.g.:

$$\cos (a + 3 \sin b)$$

This variety presumably enhances the human legibility of expressions. In Polish notation (named in honor of the Polish logician Jan Łukasiweicz), the notation is made uniform by writing all functions to precede their arguments in parentheses:

$$\cos (+(a, \times(3, \sin (b)))$$

The appeal of doing this is not obvious. However, if you now write the functions after their arguments (*reverse* Polish notation), you no longer need the parentheses:

$$b \sin 3 \times a + \cos$$

Each function takes as many of the previous (going right-to-left) results as it needs for arguments. Now the sequence is a step-by-step prescription for a human or a machine to actually evaluate the expression (assuming values are assigned to a and b). It has no syntax or extraneous symbols (parentheses), and so lends itself well to simple calculator design. All you need is a LIFO stack of registers, and functions coded to take their arguments from the stack in a LIFO fashion and return their outputs to the stack ready for the next function.

Although HP touted its first calculators as using RPN (thereby scaring off many potential customers), it was only a poor man's form of RPN— and never used to describe a *notation* but rather named a keystroke order style. The argument stack was just four registers (actually CPU registers), which limited the complexity of expressions that could be evaluated without storing intermediate results. This forced the user to take some care in finding an order of evaluation for a given expression that wouldn't overflow the stack and ruin the calculation. To further confuse things, while math functions were entered after their arguments, other calculator operations like storage and flags were entered before their arguments, e.g. STO 00 or CF 09.

Despite these shortcomings, the HP approach was reasonably simple and facilitated exploratory calculations much better than rival "algebraic" entry systems. The latter made entry of pre-determined expressions easy because keystroke sequences were more or less equivalent to the written form of the expressions. But they were miserable for combining and reusing results from previous calculations or for changing the direction of a calculation once underway. The algebraic entry enthusiasts' claim that their method let you evaluate an expression "the way it's written" was countered by Ken Newcomer, one of the early HP calculator designers, who pointed out that with HP RPN, "you don't have to write the calculation down in the first place."

The HP "RPN" used by the HP35 through the HP41C set a standard for HP calculator logic that was challenged abruptly by the HP28C in 1987, which introduced three major changes. First, the HP28C's argument stack could grow or shrink automatically and indefinitely as arguments were entered or removed, eliminating the problem of stack overflow.

Second, the syntax, or keystroke order, for all programmable commands was made uniform—all arguments, whether mathematical objects or flag numbers, register names, etc., were always entered before the commands. This meant that all arguments could be computed, and eliminated the convoluted indirect register operations and index registers needed in the older calculators. Third, "objects" on the stack were not limited to floating-point numbers, but could be of several types—real or complex numbers, matrices and vectors, symbols and expressions, and many others. This last property actually unified algebraic entry and HP RPN entry, since expressions could be keyed in as written, then evaluated (or not) with the result left on the stack for subsequent use.

Although the HP28C was a successful product, paving the way for the HP28S and the HP48/49 calculators, it didn't quite realize its designers' hopes of eliminating the *algebraic vs. RPN* feud. Even within HP there was a lot of controversy over its lack of compatibility with previous HP calculators, despite the fact that the capabilities provided by most popular HP41 programs were built into the HP28C (certainly into the HP48, which had vastly better hardware than the HP28C/S). Accustomed for many years to the HP41C-style 4-level stack and mixed-up syntax, many people found the new interface unfriendly and intimidating. (The HP42S, an updated version of the HP41C, was introduced after the HP28 as a sop to the 'old dogs'.) In the marketplace, HP calculators' reputation as 'difficult' and their premium prices restricted their success to universities and engineers, and they could not overcome HP's generally anemic marketing to dominate the mass market.

This brings us back to the original point of RPN as a poor choice of descriptor for a calculator system. What should it have been? How about *natural entry*? Think about it: when you were taught to add, you would write the numbers down on paper and then add them. That's exactly how you use an HP calculator. What could be more natural, or easier to teach? Who knows—maybe if HP had started with a kinder and gentler catchphrase like that, HP calculators would dominate the market today.

Dave Conklin began his career at HP working on the HP-41. It was Dave who offered Bill Wickes a job at HP working on calculators. Ever since, HP calculator enthusiasts have spoken of "the second Bill and Dave"—the first being Bill Hewlett and Dave Packard. Dave Conklin tells us here about work on the HP-41 design.

HP-41 DESIGN

Dave Conklin

Bernie Musch hired me into his R&D section in HP's Corvallis Division in February, 1977. I was 30 years old at the time, and had used an HP35 to get through my MS studies a few years previously. On my first day on the job, Bernie issued me an HP67 calculator and put me at a desk adjacent to his. My first assignment was to become familiar with the HP67. I read the manual from cover to cover—I was hooked immediately. I felt like I'd been hired into a toy factory.

I loved the HP67, and its printing twin, the HP97. I was thrilled to be part of the group charged with developing the successor product. The project was code-named 'coconut'. I served as the recorder for the design spec during the period in '77 and '78 when we were working out the feature set and the user interface. A central problem was how to enrich the feature set, compared with the 67/97, while at the same time making the product less intimidating to new users than the HP67 was. TI was in the process of bring the TI-59 to market; their advertising touted the algebraic user interface as a more intuitive alternative to HP's arcane RPN.

Despite my overall enthusiasm for the HP67, I personally found its keyboard, with three shift keys and keyboard legends in many colors, to be cluttered. I had trouble finding functions. I wanted to make the HP41's keyboard less cluttered, with fewer legends and fewer shift keys. At the same time we wanted to put in even more functions than the HP67 had.

I was also determined to make use of the alpha display capability to get rid of listing program steps as numeric row-column keycodes, by displaying an alphabetic name for each function. The XEQ key was invented to provide a way to invoke a function by spelling out its name. The CATalog key was invented to provide a way to remind the user of the exact names of all the built-in functions. The ASN key and USER mode were invented to provide a way for the user to customize the keyboard to his own liking. The XEQ/CAT/ASN/USER mode combination made it practical to include functions which weren't assigned to keys, and so freed us up to expand the list of functions while keeping the number of keys down to 39, only four more than the number of keys on HP's original handheld calculator. (Musch, who had been a mechanical engineer worker-bee on the HP35 development project, claimed that its model number was chosen because it had thirty-five keys.)

I recall feeling after the HP41 had been introduced that we had failed to achieve the goal of making the keyboard less intimidating than the HP67 keyboard. Now, 23 years after the product's introduction, it seems to me that the keyboard was adequately simple, and the XEQ/CAT/ASN/USER mode combination was sufficiently intuitive, to get the job done for many of our intended users. As a participant in its design, I'm a special case, but even so it may be significant that after all these years I can still pick up my HP41 and write a program on it without too much head-scratching. That I cannot do the same now on an HP48 or a TI89, despite having earned a living writing code for those machines during some of the intervening years, may be a source of amusement to my HP48 and TI89 friends. Or it might just be that we got it pretty near right on the HP41.

One of the details that we grappled with in the keyboard layout of the 41 was how to put the alphabet on the keys. In my zeal for a simpler keyboard having only a single shift key, I urged that we put the alphabet on the digit keys, three letters to a key, somewhat like a telephone keypad (except of course the top row of digits on telephones is 1-2-3, while the top row of digits on calculators is 7-8-9). My scheme was to use the same shift key for the letters as for other shifted functions, which would allow us to do a keyboard with only two legends per key. The gimmick was that to get to the second or third letter on a key, the user would press the digit key twice or three times.

During this stage of the product we made paper keyboards from A-size
sheets of paper with the outline of the keyboard. Any new idea for how
to associate functions with keys would be illustrated by writing in the
function names in the appropriate "key" boxes on the paper. This
facilitated ease-of-use comparisons—we could play as if we were using
the calculator by pressing the "keys" on the paper keyboard.

I made up a paper keyboard of the three-letters-per-digit-key proposal.
We tried entering various alpha strings, and it seemed to work OK at
first. Suppose the keyboard were set up as:

SHIFT			
	7 ABC	**8** DEF	**9** GHI
	4 JKL	**5** MNO	**6** PQR
	1 STU	**2** VWX	**3** YZ

Then to enter "ABS", the user would press:

SHIFT	7		for	**A**
SHIFT	7	7	for	**B**
SHIFT	1		for	**S**

To enter "BEEP", the user would press:

SHIFT	7	7	for		**B**
SHIFT	8	8	for the 1st		**E**
SHIFT	8	8	for the 2nd		**E**
SHIFT	6		for the		**P**

Using a shift-lock, we could eliminate the necessity to press SHIFT
between letters, so long as the letters appeared on different digit keys.
But successive letters on the same digit key, like 'A' and 'B' in the first
example, would necessitate using some key to delimit the end of the
first letter from the beginning of the next letter. Nevertheless, I was
convinced that a few extra keystrokes when entering letters was a small
price to pay to get an uncluttered keyboard.

However, when we began to try random longer words, things got a little more difficult. The whole proposal fell apart when, with Bernie looking on, I tried to spell out the word "balloon":

SHIFT	7	7		B
SHIFT	7			A
SHIFT	4	4	4	L
SHIFT	4	4	4	L
SHIFT	5	5	5	O
SHIFT	5	5	5	O
SHIFT	5	5		N

It is important to me not to leave an impression that my role in the design of the HP41 was any larger than it actually was. I was a member of the project team, and I contributed some ideas and lots of work. There were many other people involved, some, like Bernie Musch and Bill Egbert, in positions of leadership (and inspiration) far more important than mine. Bill is retired from HP now. Bernie, sadly, passed away about ten years ago. I feel fortunate to have worked with both of them and with my other project teammates, and I still get a sense of satisfaction when I use my HP41.

Diana Byrne worked on the HP48SX team with Bill Wickes. When a redesigned HP48 was planned, she became the team leader. She tells us about the challenges of upgrading the HP48S to the HP48G series of calculators. Although the HP49G has improved on the HP48G in many ways, the HP48G family is the benchmark against which most HP calculator users will compare any new graphical model—favourably, we hope.

Graphing calculator design and development

Diana Byrne

It's hard not to think about design while waiting for a flight at the Copenhagen airport. Posters of Scandinavian-designed chairs and lamps hang overhead as compact, quiet luggage carts glide across beautiful teak floors. These elegant, yet practical items are not only nice to use, they are also delightful. Many people feel this way about the traditional keys on HP calculators: they provide just the right feedback with a satisfying click.

When my team designed the software for the HP 48 G/GX and HP 38 graphing calculators, we were guided by handheld design principles as we worked to meet our project goals despite certain development constraints.

Handheld design principles are based on recognizing the important characteristics of handheld devices, understanding what needs to be optimized, and making intelligent trade-offs to deal with the inherent limitations of handheld devices.

Handheld devices have these characteristics:

- they are low cost and portable, and thus personal
- they are good for back-of-the-envelope types of explorations
- they do something that is not easy to do on paper or in your head (such as complicated calculations or zooming in on a graph)

- they support an asymmetric flow of information (also known as key-per-function), since a small amount of input from the user results in a lot of information back from the device

- they just work, and have almost no maintenance requirements, because of their focused functionality.

HP calculator design goals evolved as the target markets changed. Earlier HP calculators were designed primarily for engineers, so next-bench design worked well. As more features were added, calculators such as the HP 28 and HP 48 series became toolkits for engineers, and were especially useful for engineering students who need to learn a variety of engineering techniques while in school. Most professional engineers only use a small fraction of the functionality in an HP calculator, but which functions they use varies from engineer to engineer. So, by designing for engineering students, the aggregate needs of professional engineers are also met.

HP's migration into the education market started with engineering students, then moved to college mathematics, advanced-placement calculus, and other high-school mathematics and science courses. One of the main design goals for the HP 48G/GX was to add a dialogue-box-style graphical user interface to make it easier to use for students and teachers. But we also wanted to maintain the advanced user interface, where arguments are placed on the stack, an operation is selected from a soft-key menu, and then the results are returned to the stack. So we created a dual user interface with green keys for the new dialogue boxes and purple keys for the traditional stack-based user interface.

Displaying the graph of a function, then being able to trace, zoom in, and explore the graph is the 'killer app' that made calculators so popular in mathematics classes. The main design goal for the HP 38 was to create a graphing calculator for pre-calculus mathematics students and teachers. It was originally intended to be a platform for small applications (called aplets) that could be delivered over the Internet to the HP 38 and used as educational activities in the classroom. The HP 38 aplet platform was designed for exploring mathematical functions using graphic, symbolic, and numeric representations. These are the "three views" promoted by the National Council of Teachers of Mathematics.

Working with Singapore on the HP 38 project introduced a whole new set of development constraints that we did not have on the previous HP 48 G/GX project. When the HP calculator line was moved to Singapore, most of my team still wanted to work on calculators, but did not want to relocate. So we added Singapore engineers and formed a geographically-distributed team.

We worked hard at team-building activities and maintaining multiple forms of communication. At the start of the project, the Singapore engineers came to Oregon for over a month so we could get to know each other. We all worked on developing our virtual meeting skills by practicing with everyone in the same location to begin with. The other people in the Corvallis office thought it was strange when we held meetings with each of us sitting in our own cubicle, in front of our own computer with a telephone headset. The web, originally designed for just this purpose of supporting geographically-distributed work groups, was critical to our success. We used the then-new Mosaic web browser, and we all learned to write HTML documents to keep in touch. We also relied on an instant-messenger style program called "talk" to see who else was on line and up for a phone call despite the eight-hour time difference.

The Oregon part of the team also traveled to Singapore. We had already heard about Singapore culture from our team members, but it was still a bit of a shock to encounter the customs form handed out on the airplane before landing in Singapore. On one side, it said "Welcome to Singapore" in friendly-looking script. On the other side, in bold red letters, it said "Death to Drug Traffickers".

Well, got to go now and catch my flight. I've just been to the international conference on Wireless and Mobile Technologies in Education. These days, wireless has come to many classrooms (and the Copenhagen airport) and I'm still working to bring well-designed handheld technology to teachers and students. Many of the same

handheld design principles still apply, although the players have
changed as HP has receded, while mobile phones and wireless PDAs are
the next big little thing.

PERSPECTIVES

We have described how the club developed, and how HP calculator design advanced. Let us see how a few people with particular viewpoints saw the story from somewhat different perspectives.

Neville Joseph became the club's second Chairman. Unlike most members, he uses HP handhelds mainly for business purposes, not technical ones. Like other members, he sees clubs as fulfilling an important role, regardless of the use to which the calculators are put.

Users' clubs

Neville Joseph (77)

I am a great believer in users clubs. I joined them for every computer I have owned, and was a member of the original HP club in the U.S. (although I later realised that this was a commercial venture rather than a club, which—in UK parlance—is a club owned by all its members).

I think that I learned about HPCC from the U.S. newsletter. I can't think of any other reason that I was only member #77—obviously the founders did not know my interests and I did not know them.

It is difficult for us now to appreciate the state of the computer industry at that time. Programming had an excitement, and low-level programming was the sort of thing that kept addicts up to 6 o'clock in the morning. But computers were expensive, and the only ones available for hobbyists were toys suitable for playing games, but not for serious thought.

HP were the first company to market complicated calculators (i.e., those which could do more than $+ - \times \div$ and $\sqrt{}$). All calculators are actually computers, but the owner is limited to the interface provided by the manufacturer's program. With programmable calculators, the manufacturer's program not only provided number entry, simple manipulations and a display, but also provided a high-level language.

Some of the members of HPCC discovered how to get into the manufacturer's program—how it worked, how it used internal temporary storage (RAM), and how to use the low-level instructions to do things differently from the way the manufacturer offered. Examples included faster instructions, and things which were not normally allowed because if wrongly used they might do damage, either to the user's figures by leaving out credibility checks (which typically take up far more than actual calculation time) or to the machine itself (e.g., by switching on a print head but not switching it off).

To give them credit, at that time HP (unlike most manufacturers) did not actively prevent this activity. They would not spare resources to support such use, but they would not go out of their way to stop it, and would even provide some internal documents to assist users who wanted more than was officially available. This was very brave—these were not documents intended for the public, and the internal jokes were unprofessional, as were some of the comments along the lines of: "this seems to duplicate another flag, but we aren't sure if the first flag does something else, so we use another one just in case."

But the real joy of the low-level programming which could be done on calculators was that they were affordable; 'real' computers were far beyond ordinary hobby spending capacity. My first computer was bought for me by a grateful client who had had one year's profit disappear from the Inland Revenue's sight by a loophole which no longer exists. "What would you do with such wealth?" he asked me, and I said I would buy a computer, so he gave me one—keyboard, one line numeric display, thermal strip printer (one number per line) and HP BASIC with, I think, 800 bytes of RAM. After that, I never looked back!

Nowadays, almost anyone can afford a computer, or at least have access to one. A range of programming languages is freely available from macro languages provided as part of the package up to freeware versions of C. The excitement is no longer there. And if you want to program in Windows, the initial entry fee (in terms of learning time and details to be mastered) is substantial. Besides, where is the fun in working within someone else's program which keeps you away from the hardware and only offers you a huge range of subroutine calls which must be used strictly in accordance with rules which have little interest in themselves? This is why HPCC still survives, even though programming calculators faces stiff competition from full-sized machines.

Sadly, HP made so much money on printers that they lost interest in calculators, and gave away the lead they had to follow the Intel/ Windows/WindowsCE bandwagon. I was caught up in this—I have a Jornada 720 and all I can say is, don't buy one. Thaddeus are still selling 200LXs—grab one before they all go.

And if you want to experience the thrill of low-level programming on a big machine, I recommend Forth. This is virtually the high-level language offered by HP on its calculators, but under MSDOS it combines high- and low-level programming power—just as our club members do on calculators; use high level for simplicity but drop down to low level when speed or extra facilities are wanted. Bring excitement back into computers! (And yes, Forth does have a users' group.)

As Rabin mentioned, hardware hacking was one of the main games at PPC-UK. Sadly, we have to report that hacking is no longer a major activity in the club, though some members continue to hack and share their discoveries and achievements. Among computer users, "hacking" generally means understanding a computer system so well that one can modify it, or exploit its features usefully. The pejorative use of "hacker" to mean a person breaking into a system (originally telephone systems) came later. Here Gary Friedman recalls some hardware hacking feats from the great days of PPC.

A HARDWARE HACKER'S PERSPECTIVE

GARY FRIEDMAN

I won my first HP calculator at an electronic design competition at UCLA (University of California, Los Angeles) in 1980. It was an HP-41, an incredibly powerful computer that was far ahead of the rest of the world. (As a reference point, my high school was still teaching how to use slide rules in the first weeks of its chemistry class!) Being an engineering major, and not owning a personal computer, this little wonder was like a godsend—I could do any required calculations in less than half the time it took those losers who owned TI calculators, and, because of its humble calculator-like exterior, it provided me with a significant competitive advantage while completing my engineering courses.

It may be unhealthy to be in love with a calculator, but during my college days that is probably how it appeared: I carried it everywhere, usually on my belt loop, and used it for everything. Using the time module, it became my customized alarm clock (with an eleven-minute snooze cycle) which would wake me up at different times depending on the day of the week. I had programs that kept a phone book, calculated sunset times (for my photography), emulated the HP 16C, and even solved the Rubik's Cube. Using synthetic instructions, I created a Hangman game program which I played with the elementary school students I was tutoring at the time.

My most-used utility was a quick polynomial root finder. And I never, never had to worry about anyone asking to borrow my calculator, for if they did, exactly thirteen seconds would elapse before I heard the inevitable phrase: "Where's the equals?"

And I'll never forget my first PPC meeting. A very soft-spoken individual came up to me and handed me a piece of paper with two numbers on it. "That is the smallest number pair which, when divided, will result in your phone number!" Later, I learned that this person was Clifford Stern, a famous and regular contributor to the journal. That evening I also met Richard Nelson ("Fearless Leader") and Joseph K. Horn, a priest for whom exploring algorithms was sheer entertainment. I realized then that I had joined a club which attracted some very intelligent and unique people.

Unlike the vast majority of PPC members, I was also adept at hardware as well as software, and relished in the opportunity to merge the two. The first thing I did, after talking with folks who knew, was to take the calculator apart and double the clock speed by simply by-passing one capacitor. This proved to be a valuable lesson in engineering tolerances when, during a final exam on a very, very hot summer's day, the calculator crashed. (Did I mention it was a closed-book, closed-note exam and I secretly had all the formulas I was supposed to memorize in extended memory?) The next day I installed a switch that could slow the machine back down again as required. ☺

With the advent of the Hewlett Packard Interface Loop (HP-IL) and the 16-bit port IL Converter ("82166A" for those of you who love HP's nomenclature), real world I/O was possible, and I ended up writing more than a dozen "hardware project" articles for the *PPC Journal*. In one article, I hooked up my 41 to my 35mm camera so I could take night-time "time exposure" images, bracketing in ½-stop increments, while I stayed warm inside. In another, I completely automated my photographic darkroom using my 41—from negative analyzer to enlarger timer to developer/bath timer. This allowed me to concentrate on creative darkroom pursuits instead of being consumed by the 'dog work'.

For my final project before earning a degree in Electrical Engineering, I turned my 41 into an interactive telephone answering machine, complete with speech synthesis and Touch Tone® decoding.

When the HP71 was introduced, I immediately took it apart and brought some unused CPU lines to the outside. Burying myself in the 71 IDS manuals and teaching myself how to program in Saturn assembly language, I distinctly remember the moment when I successfully produced an 18 kHz square wave using a simple loop in assembly language: I was sitting in the passenger seat of a car, en route to the PPC club meeting! (Fortunately, I also had a battery-powered Tektronix oscilloscope with me to measure the frequency of the square wave produced!) Later on I used this CPU-control-of-I/O-lines technique to hook the 71 up to a Polaroid Ultrasonic Transducer so I could measure the distance to things by bouncing sound off of them and timing the echo's return.

I also used the 71 in the heart of an intelligent telephone autodialer (it would recognize a busy signal and automatically redial), and to control multimedia shows, including a "dissolve unit" controlling the light intensity of two slide projectors using pulse-width modulation of the AC signal. Many *PPC Journal* articles followed, explaining the circuitry and the software to control all these cutting-edge hardware projects. Fame and fortune followed. (Well, fame anyway.) All of this was eventually rolled into a book, *Control the World with HP-IL*, published in 1987.

For me, this was a very exciting time, because in a world which was dominated by large, immobile, clunky, takes-five-minutes-to-boot-up (things don't change, do they?) DOS-based IBM PCs, I was playing with Hewlett Packard's little wonders which were powerful, portable, completely self-contained development systems. They were far ahead of their time in terms of form factor, power consumption, user interface, number crunching abilities, and programmability—the HP-71 could be programmed in three different language environments, all of which could call each other! And while the rest of the world was impressed with one parallel and one serial port that came with their bulky PCs, HP's innovative HP-IL interface could allow my pocket device to access up to 960 connected peripherals simultaneously!

What enthralled me most about working with the HP handheld
computers is that this was my first inkling that technology could
actually set you free. The vast majority of what I built could be carried
with me and used anywhere. (The 41-based camera controller, for
example, continues to have a place in my camera bag, ready to do work
for me while I am far from civilization.) I could set it up as a data
logger and have it wake up, take a measurement, and shut off again all
on its own. Because all the IL peripherals ran on batteries, the controller
could power up all peripheral devices, print something out, save some
data to tape, and shut everything off again until the next measurement
cycle. All the units had their own keyboard and display, so software
development and testing could be done interactively, without a bulky
and constraining development system. And since it was an open-ended
interface, there was virtually no limit to the amount of I/O that could
be performed with this handheld device—just add another peripheral or
16-bit parallel port to the loop! Compared to the non-portable, power-
hungry, limited I/O Personal Computer, HP's calculators were light
years ahead of the accepted world standard.

Much has changed since those exciting days. Hewlett Packard has
changed course in their calculator strategy many times; first dropping
I/O in favor of sophisticated symbolic manipulation, then dropping
symbolic manipulation in favor of 4-bangers with an equals key.
Calculator operations moved from Corvallis to Singapore to Australia
to Middle Earth. Spreadsheets and more powerful symbolic math
processors running on PCs took over as the professionals' tools of
choice. The era in which a person could get excited about a serious,
number-crunching calculator is rapidly drawing to a close. Today, when
someone mentions a handheld computer, for example, they now
automatically think of a Palm Pilot!

That is why the book which you are reading now has been compiled—
to document, in an easily-digestible way, the worldwide phenomena of
the handheld calculator clubs and the culture, activities, and values
which grew from it. Like the slide rule and the Jedi Light Saber before
it, the HP calculator is a long-forgotten tool that demanded dedication

and self-training from its user to be used effectively—it became an extension of the user, because the user was such an integral part of the system. To this day, HP handhelds remain unrivaled in terms of portability, versatility, expandability, and power consumption. And although the calculators which once brought us all together are now a piece of forgotten history, the original mantra they carried continues to this day:

Technology can set us free. Imagination can make us soar.

How Raan Young worked hard to get into HP calculator development—and then worked hard on the development team—is a story of American youth at the time. But it is also a story of how HP handhelds were developed in the great old days.

PORTRAIT OF THE ENGINEER AS A YOUNG NERD

RAAN YOUNG

June 1972 I was, euphemistically, a student worker in the University of Washington's Physiology and Biophysics department. I say "euphemistically" because, like many a child of the '60s, my path through college was convoluted (to say the least). While I started college in 1968 as an honors Math student, by 1972 it was no longer clear if I was a student at all. Politics and other distractions of the late '60s had taken their toll, and in 1972 my job at the P-Bio department consisted of helping them meet their obligations to various granting agencies by accounting for the equipment they had purchased.

On this particular day, I was looking for a new piece of equipment one of the professors had just acquired—something called a "Hewlett-Packard HP-35 Electronic Slide Rule". Being a good nerd, I owned my share of slide rules. I'd been building electronic gadgets since high school. I'd had more than a passing exposure to computers (as much as you could get in the days when they lived in big, air-conditioned, locked rooms). I'd even spent one high-school summer crunching data on a typewriter-sized Friden electronic desktop calculator (CRT display and 4-level RPN stack). But what the heck was an "Electronic Slide Rule"?

I still remember the sense of rapture I felt when the professor showed me his HP-35 and I realized this was something with more computing power than that Friden desktop—and I was holding it in my *hand!* I was hooked! I wanted one! But $400 was almost four months rent on my house—there was no way I was going to get my own HP-35...

I look back now and recognize that moment as a life-changing event. Somewhere in the back of my mind, the seed was planted. I wanted to be part of the world that had brought that machine into existence.

Fast-forward to the summer of 1974. I had parlayed my student job, tracking equipment for the P-Bio department, into a full-time UW staff position in the office responsible for equipment management campus-wide. I was still tracking down equipment for accounting, but now I had keys to every room on campus and the items for which I searched ranged from desks to nuclear reactors to an HP-65...

Say what?! Suddenly I remembered that "epiphany" with the HP-35. But the HP-65 was much more—it was programmable! You could store the programs on magnetic cards! This was amazing! It was a computer you could carry around on your belt! And at $800, it was also out of my league. But now I knew—I was going to be part of that world somehow!

By 1975, I had been promoted to management, in charge of the team who tracked down the University's equipment. I was also back in school, taking advantage of the UW staff benefit of one class free per quarter. I had saved my pennies and HP had made life a little easier; they introduced the HP-55 at $400. With the rationalization that "I need it for school", I bought my first HP calculator!

Its memory could only hold 50 steps, and you had to re-enter each different program every time you wanted to use it, but I finally had my own programmable calculator! I spent hours writing programs and learning every nuance of that calculator. It was the doorway to a new world and a new life, and I never looked back.

In mid-1976, I was busy redefining my UW job—the University was replacing its 1960-era inventory software with something up to date, featuring on-line, real-time data access and nightly updates. Nobody else in the office understood what that meant, but I saw the path to the future clearly now, and I knew this was an opportunity to take it—I turned myself into a systems analyst. I started working with the inventory software vendor and I taught myself COBOL programming, using a Burroughs reference manual. I worked late into the night, hunched over a "portable" teletype I had borrowed, connected via a 110-baud modem to the big Burroughs 6700 used for the UW's administrative computing.

The love of programming inspired by that HP-55 carried me on as I journeyed further and further into this new world of computers. But the HP-55 was getting a bit short on computing power in the light of my new knowledge, and I decided to plunk down another $450 and upgrade to the newly-introduced HP-67 (even then, it was becoming clear that computers would never qualify as a good investment). That HP-67 is still one of my favorite HP calculators. I think it is the most aesthetically pleasing calculator HP ever made, and it carried me through the next 3 years of school, providing countless opportunities for entertainment.

The HP-67 also introduced me to the world of calculator fanatics—the PPC. There were actually other people around who were as passionate about these things as I was. Amazing! Not only were they stretching the programming limits of these calculators, they were delving into the inner workings and learning things that I could never have imagined! I knew I had found something special.

My discovery of the PPC was the result of a meeting for calculator fans, advertised in the UW student newspaper. I was intrigued, and I went to the meeting. The talk that night was about the newly discovered ability to get inside the HP-67's memory and introduce instruction codes that were not intended by HP's developers. Fascinating! I promptly became an active member of the UW club, joined PPC immediately (#2545) and bought every back issue—I had a lot of reading to do. I remained a member of PPC until its demise in 1985. Richard Nelson, and the club he led, played a significant role in the path to my next move…

In 1979 I graduated with a BSEE from the UW, and interviewed with the Corvallis Division of Hewlett-Packard (HP having moved its calculator business to Corvallis only a couple of years earlier). I knew that was where I wanted to be, and I didn't even bother to interview for another job. In May of 1979 I became the first PPC member to be hired by HP (HP-wide as far as I know, and certainly for the calculator division).

I was on the inside looking out! Best of all, I'd never have to buy another HP calculator! This proved to be both a false and a true expectation—false because I have purchased HP calculators since then as collector items; true for reasons that would not become apparent for several years...

My arrival in the promised land coincided nicely with the introduction of the HP-41C—a "calculator" that was the epitome of the magic that had led me there. The HP-41 and its follow-ons were truly computers you could wear on your belt. With expandable memory, plug-in software ROMs, and eventually the addition of HP-IL and all the associated peripheral devices, the distinction between calculator and computer had blurred beyond recognition. Though the

The HP calculator family in 1998
Photo by Hewlett Packard

41 family was never one of my official projects, I adopted this machine as my hobby and invested significant time in exploring various modifications, "accessories", and software discoveries. I also got very good at displaying the infamous HP "poker face" when fellow PPC members asked me probing questions...

While I played with the HP-41, my real job was being one of the software designers on the HP-75—Kangaroo! This was a completely new approach to the "small and powerful machine" obsession I had come to know. Our task was to pack all the functionality of the HP-85 desktop BASIC computer into a machine that you could carry easily. Not quite on your belt, but still portable and definitely a computer; one of the earliest laptops, if you will. Besides creating many aspects of the machine itself, my penchant for play resulted in the APRIL ROM and its official descendent, the I/O ROM. Both of these contained hidden functions and messages for the PPC aficionado, a nod to my roots.

The HP-75 project was the most fun I ever had while at HP. Some of the people I worked with on that project are still my best friends to this day. As the years went by, I came to understand how unique and special the elements and environment of that first project were. But the HP-75 was not the instant success that we all believed it would be. The team split up and went in various directions—after producing the I/O ROM and helping with the HP-75D/pod follow-on, I started looking around for something new.

In 1984, MS-DOS and Unix were both beginning to make significant impressions on the future of computing, and it didn't take long to figure out which camp had more appeal to my sense of aesthetics. I decided to move into the support end of the computer world and create a lab computing environment that would free my fellow software engineers from the arcane development tools we had been forced to work with—I became a Unix *guru*. It seemed that the "powerful" part of "small and powerful machine" was becoming more important than "small"; yet, I knew that some day the two would come together again.

While I was no longer officially involved in the development of products coming from the "calculator" division (this designation became less and less accurate), I continued to play and make contributions, behind the scenes, to the HP-48, HP-95, HP-100, and HP-200. By the early 1990s "small" and "powerful" again came together at HP, in the form of some of the most innovative laptop computers ever produced. But many other changes had occurred at HP as well, and I watched what seemed to be a repeated pattern of abandonment applied to each innovative new product. Time after time, HP threw away a product that seemed to me to be unique and poised to capture a new, budding market. The vision that had produced those first amazing machines seemed gone and forgotten. Time passed, and dreams moved elsewhere. Sadly, my expectation of never having to buy another HP calculator came true—HP no longer made the kind of machines that inspired that fanatical devotion.

The HP of 1997 was not the HP that I had joined in 1979 and when the Mobile Computing Division (as the calculator division came to be known) decided that it no longer needed a lab-supported development environment, I decided it was time to test my dream of being independent. I left HP and started my own consulting company.

Now, 5 years later, MCD is going through a final meltdown and there is nothing left of the lineage that traces back to that first group of developers in the Advanced Products Division, who built those machines that started me down this road.

These days I do consulting work for Unix and Windows—software design, system/network administration, security, and the occasional 100kW laser repair. The passion I discovered in 1972 still guides me, though its form is now more complex—"small and powerful" is a moving target.

And there are still an inordinate number of HP calculators lying around my office. Sometimes, I'll pick one of those machines up and think about an idea for a program. If only there were more time—life, and programming, was so much more simple in the old days…

At the start of the 1980s, personal programmable calculators were the only way ordinary people could have their own computers. The IBM Personal Computer had not yet been introduced. A variety of other personal computers did already exist, beginning with the Apple I. CP/M provided a common operating system for most, but each had its own foibles—and most were too expensive for the average user to be convinced to pay for one. The programmable calculators from HP and TI were more affordable, and very portable. Hewlett Packard even had a display of them in the entrance to the plant where calculators were developed and made, in Corvallis, Oregon. This corridor was popularly known as "The Hall of Fame".

My walk along
the Hall of Fame

Jim Donnelly

For many years, one of the highlights of any calculator enthusiast's visit to the HP Corvallis site was a walk along the "Hall of Fame". The Hall of Fame was a series of mounted product models arranged by family in rough chronological order. Each product was labeled with its model number, internal nickname and date of introduction.

The Hall of Fame meant many things to the people who saw it. My favorite memories of the Hall of Fame are of HP employees who brought their families onto the site for a tour. Passing by, I heard fragments of their descriptions of the products, and sometimes a few words about their role in the making of the product: "This was my favorite project", "there was going to be another like this one, but they cancelled it" (HP 95C), "I put battery clips in thousands of these", or "this was the first to have a card reader". And so on.

For calculator club members, the Hall of Fame became an interesting form of time-line, where members could chronicle their interest in calculators. During club meetings, a frequent phrase heard during introductions was: "I starting programming HP calculators with the HP-XX." I remember seeing small groups of club members pointing to panels on the Hall of Fame to show where they got their start with calculators.

Looking back on the sixteen years I spent with HP's handheld products, I've come to realize that my walk down the Hall of Fame started very early. In 1972, my father bought the first HP 35 calculator ever sold. When he brought the calculator home, I was doing homework for a slide rule class. In an instant, I realized that my world was never going to be the same. I was stunned to see difficult calculations, interpolations, and approximations reduced to a few keystrokes. I look at that moment as the beginning of my journey along the time scale represented by the Hall of Fame.

Walking from left to right down the Hall of Fame from the HP 35 to the HP 48GX, there were places that represented significant points of evolution in technologies, products, the lives of our customers, and my life as well. After the HP-65 calculator was introduced, the community of people who devoted significant portions of their lives to HP calculators grew quickly. As a college student, I couldn't afford an HP calculator, and was very envious of those who had them. One of my father's colleagues had an HP 65, and made a hobby of submitting programs to the Users' Library. He took pride in his large number of submissions. This was my first glimpse of the interest in calculators that was spreading around the world, and what contributed to the formation of users clubs.

Just before I joined HP, a friend had purchased an HP 41C, and my little circle of friends spent an evening at a pizza parlor going through its capabilities. The waitresses were bemused by the circle of "nerds" surrounding a small beeping calculator. Perhaps this was my first taste of what users club meetings would be like in the future.

When I joined HP, the Hall of Fame was years away, but my awareness of the march of innovation was heightened by a series of plaques in the hallway showing the progress of integrated circuit development. They showed the progress in the number of transistors on a chip, the number of chips on a wafer, etc.. Clearly, HP wasn't standing still, and the newer parts were ever more complex. Some of those plaques are still on display in Corvallis.

My awareness of the users clubs sharpened quickly. I found out fairly quickly that contributors to the Users' Library and members of the calculator clubs put a great deal of thought and critique into their views of HP's products. Over the years, I'm very sure that these people's

insights influenced my design choices as I worked on products destined
for the Hall of Fame.

After the Hall of Fame was installed, it was immensely gratifying to see
products that I worked on hanging on the wall. For me, the most
significant part of my relationship with HP calculators were the legions
of other HP people and customers that I got to meet, learn from, and
work with. When I looked at products along the Hall of Fame, images
of the people associated with those products came quickly to mind.

Some products never appeared along the Hall of Fame. There just
wasn't as much interest in putting up application ROM modules. Some
of the modules I would have nominated for the Hall of Fame were
notable for elegance, significant capabilities that advanced the product
line, or both. My personal nominations would include the Petroleum
Fluids Pac for the HP 41C, which introduced unit management, and the
Math Pac for the HP 71, which provided the foundation of the math
code for many products. I was delighted when my most favorite of all
projects in my career at HP—the HP Solve Equation Library card for
the HP 48SX—appeared in the Hall of Fame.

Some Users' Library contributors and calculator club members
contributed very directly to products appearing on the Hall of Fame. I
have fond memories of many late nights working on the Equation
Library card while Frank Wales and Włodek Mier-Jędrzejowicz were
working on the HP 41 Emulator card. Frank worked on code, and
Włodek worked on the manual. During this time I was also working on
my first HP 48 Handbook. We exchanged many war stories and tales of
debugging agonies during those times. Since we were all night-owls, we
were sometimes the only people working in that huge HP building.

Today, the Hall of Fame is gone, but my memories of the Hall of Fame,
the products, and the people around the world who were associated with
them, remain a poignant reminder of a great phase in my time with HP.

CODA

HPCC continues to hold meetings and conferences, to publish *Datafile* and provide a web site. But members are increasingly apprehensive about HP's future direction in handheld computing. Handheld computers like the Jornada were seen as an alternative to calculators, but the Jornada family has been shut down too. We watch the end of an era, and wonder if there will be a future era with room for "Beep" in it.

John Olwoch has been enthusiastic user of HP-41 and HP48 calculators for many years. As he writes here, he wonders where HP might take him next—if anywhere.

THE END OF AN ERA

JOHN OLWOCH (700)

The Club

Way back in 1984, I bought my first HP calculator, an HP41C. It was a nice, solid machine; a constant companion. I fondly remember spending a whole weekend going through the manual, trying out the examples. I recall finding a membership application form for HPCC, but did nothing about it. The next machine I wanted was an HP71B: this, however, was a bit too expensive for my modest pay packet.

Fast-forward to 1990, and the 48SX. I found an advert of this beauty in an electronics magazine and wanted one. I had only recently bought an Amiga 500 computer and enjoyed some sleepless nights tapping away on the keys and marvelling at the superb graphics. The urge to get the 48SX was, however, too strong, so the Amiga had to go. When I went to buy the machine, I asked the shop assistant to give me a demo. He just laughed and handed it to me. I came across the HPCC membership form again and this time thought: "why not?" So began my association with the club.

The meetings were full of life. Anyone passing by and looking in would immediately know what was going on—geeks and nerds unite. The enthusiasm of the club was infectious and uplifting. There would be little groups all round the room, chatting away, squirting programs into each others machines. Programming the 48SX was a joy; I think I managed five programs and articles for *Datafile* that year. My association with the club proved fruitful because it later led to a job with Graeme Cawsey at Tuscan Consultants. I had a great time there.

Such enthusiasm as there was doesn't seem to appear anymore. Could it be because there appears to be nothing exciting on the HP front? A stranger entering the room wouldn't guess we were a computer club. I find myself going to fewer and fewer meetings. In the past, I always looked forward to the meetings, even if it meant enduring traffic jams and other irritations along the way. Now I find myself looking for excuses not to go. I've watched numbers fall—the current member pack has the names of all members on one page. "What will it be like next year?" I wonder.

The Machines

I'm not an expert on all the machines—try Włodek—but I know a good machine when I see one. All the calculators, up to the 48GX, have been excellent machines. The 49G's hardware is too 'me too-ish' for my liking, trying to be all things to all people. I've no idea about the Jornadas, nor do I have any interest in them. What made the HP machines stand out from the rest of the competition, apart from the solid, unique designs, were the 'little extras' that were available. A big plus for me was the connectivity and storage. From a programmer's point of view, my preference is for the 48SX/GX. Being a Forth fan, I especially like the RPL language.

I always kept an open ear for news of new machines on the horizon. When I got wind of the 'Xpander', I was all ears, eagerly awaiting its arrival, but it wasn't to be. All ready for production then – *poof!* – gone with the wave of the corporate wand. So too went 'Calypso'.

When I checked the HPCC web site recently, I had to pause. One can't laugh and do other things at the same time. What did I find? A questionnaire asking what we want in a calculator, what are our favourite features, etc.. The Corvallis team was broken up, so was ACO in Australia, probably the best calculator engineers they'll ever get. Two machines dropped just before production. Are we supposed to think our views are going to make the slightest bit of difference? Ha! I assume no machines are made without extensive market research. What then went wrong with these latest two? It would seem to me, to paraphrase Mr

Spock (*The Wrath Of Khan*) as he lay dying: "The needs of the shareholders far outweigh the needs of the enthusiasts..."

I still hunger for handheld programmable machines. I have two Palms. These are great for programming, especially with the 'Quartus Forth' package. Lately, I've had my eyes on the Sharp SL-5500, a Linux handheld to complement my Linux box. Would I buy a Jornada? No! Same too for the iPaq.

Last Thoughts

Will club membership continue to fall? Probably. Maybe. With the calculator future on the HP horizon looking bleak, we should be opening up to other machines. After all, it is supposed to be the *Handheld* and *Portable Computer* Club, not the *HP* Computer Club, as Bob Pulluard points out (*Datafile* V21 N4). Perhaps references to HP should be dropped from the front of *Datafile*, and the constitution, as a first step.

There may be new machines in future. These will most probably be 'me-too' machines for corporate coat pockets. Sadly and truly, the end of an era.

We began this book with HP's own "Thank you, Beep...!" article. That was a science fiction story, not an attempt to predict the future exactly. It stands first as a story about a user of a handheld computer of the future, and uses science fiction themes of its time to provide the background. Yet it is interesting to compare the technology assumed in the story with current trends.

Can we hope that HP will yet make a true "Beep"?

Half a Beep

Włodek Mier-Jędrzejowicz (9)

Half-way between the writing of the story and its setting, how far are we towards the technologies described by the author? Gordon Dickson was a well-known science fiction writer, and he used assumptions of his day in writing the story. The difference was that the HP computer was the hero.

The computing power, and storage capacity, suggested in the story are indeed reasonable expectations based on current trends. Colour screens are already at least as good as the one suggested in the story and shown in the pictures that accompanied its original appearance. Voice recognition is also advancing towards the level suggested; the main difficulty is likely to be a social one—the level of background noise. Acceptable voice output is also available even now. Whether artificial intelligence and computing power will develop sufficiently to allow a machine such as *Beep* to understand sentences and participate in conversations is far less clear. The joke: "it may be artificial, but it's not intelligent" still applies to AI at present levels. Even if artificial intelligence and the ability to speak *do* develop over coming years, there may be a psychological problem: will people want to have electronic boxes they can talk to, and that seem as smart as the owner?

A different question is that of the communications and data infrastructure assumed by the story. Communications between handheld devices and networks is easily available already—by radio, not infra-red links as in the story—but there is an assumption that intelligent databases and communications systems would allow *Beep* to order tickets, and have lost items forwarded. Some of this is profitable—fully automated ticket sales, for example—but would companies pay to set up automated forwarding of lost luggage? If they would, why have they not made luggage delivery less error-prone already?

In any case, would it still be necessary to carry paper? Again, this is a question both of technology and of human nature. "Smart paper" is being developed: a single thin and flexible sheet that is sensitive to writing (but can distinguish writing from folding or flexing), displays a selected page, and allows writing added to that page to be stored and displayed with it, or erased. People might prefer to carry a single sheet of smart paper together with a storage medium for it. But would that be accepted as the basis of legal documents? Paper documents can be forged, but faking an electronic document is currently much easier. Maybe it will not be by the time of the story, in which case our business traveller would not have papers to be lost.

Technologies such as intelligent computers (or smart paper) presently use a lot of electrical power. HP's first handhelds required frequent recharging of their batteries, until lower-power circuitry was introduced with the HP-41. Battery power and long life are the norm for handheld calculators, even powerful graphical ones, and for low-power handheld computers such as the HP-95LX and its successors. Unfortunately, current palm computers use fast processors and have reverted to the need for frequent battery charging. *Beep* seems to have little problem with this—will sufficiently low-power processors and memory become available? Or will battery technology have advanced sufficiently for a handheld to pack enough power for days of use? A battery with that much power stored in it would actually be a potential risk; it might even be possible to use it as an explosive device.

Which brings us to the matter of travel. Gordon Dickson assumed that there would be little evidence of security checks; but he had not heard of September 11, 2001. Maybe security can be made efficient and secure again by the time of the story, or maybe travel will not be as smooth. As for speed, he assumed that spaceplanes would be available by the time of his story. Spaceplanes are indeed being developed, but only slowly, and it seems more likely that our businessman would be flying in a Boeing Sonic Cruiser—or maybe one of the coming

European giant passenger planes. Or will fuel costs have risen so far by the time of the story, due to shortages, wars or environmental taxes, that the trip would not take place at all, and *Beep* would instead arrange a virtual meeting with other people's *Beeps*?

Would those other people be male? It is not clear whether the author *assumed* that a business traveller of the time would be male, or whether he arbitrarily chose a man for the story. Even when he wrote the story, some people would have accused him of being sexist in its assumptions!

One final assumption: *Beep* is an HP handheld. This assumes that HP will still exist, and will still be making personal computers, rather than cameras or smart paper. After all, Pan Am ceased to trade a few years after Stanley Kubrick showed a Pan Am shuttle in the film *2001: A Space Odyssey*. But then, Gordon Dickson wrote "Thank you, Beep…!" for HP, so he could hardly have done otherwise. And if HP commissioned a story about a device such as *Beep*, let us hope they intend to build it when the time comes.

For years, Jeremy has been commenting on HP's handheld technology, and making uncannily accurate predictions about it.

Perhaps, in 2038, we shall be using not a Beep but a waitron.

HP – There is no sequel

Jeremy Smith (185)

Actually, my involvement with calculators was in trying to fulfil their 'promise', and the fun I had doing it. The promise of calculators was marketing spiel I heard from one of the main marketing guys at the Corvallis calculator conference in 1981. He was basically saying that the calculator could do many things (calculate complex problems and run sophisticated programs) and that many imminent add-ons would make it even more useful and powerful (HP-IL and all the devices).

I took much of that literally, and built up in my mind a sense of what might be called the 'computational model' of 'life, the universe and everything', the idea that many aspects of life's problems can usefully be explored by modelling on a computer, and not just strictly mathematical and engineering problems. This was thrilling in two ways. Firstly, the calculator goes in your pocket, and therefore is a constant companion, a handy device that at the push of a few buttons delivers instant answers, as well as being ready to store and capture information as it's happening. Secondly, since the machine (HP 41 at that time) predated the IBM PC, it was indeed a viable, valid state-of-the-art computer.

As should be quite apparent, I was imbuing the machine with far more than anyone knew it was capable of. But that didn't matter. I went on to explore vast worlds that I never knew existed. For example, I wanted to describe simple 3D scenes and do virtual fly-bys. Since the calculator just had a text screen, this meant viewing the results on a funky little thermal printer, but I discovered the complex world of 3D graphics. And so I got to explore many problems by banging away on the machine trying to wheedle out answers.

Two important aspects arose from this. One is that, probably 90% of
our computer time was spent building tools to make the machine work,
and only 10% on actually solving problems. Kind of like building a
workshop in order to do crafts, but you find that most of your time is
spent refining the workshop and its tools so that you can do the craft
more ably. I'll call it the overheads problem.

The other aspect is the community. The club brought together many
people all as equally enthusiastic and also having fun tackling problems.
And so we'd share, compete, and challenge one another. Problems
mostly in the 90% set were easy to define and solve discretely. Libraries
were built (for example, PPC ROM), and the promise of a new machine
was always on the horizon.

But I always wanted to get back to the non-overheads problem, the ideal
of the machine being an invisible part of me such that I could be a
super hero with my secret universe in a hidden box that I could
suddenly brandish from the folds of my cloak to solve the problem at
hand. Many things conspired against this impossible ideal. The amount
of work to prepare it for any particular task was quite huge. Although
the machines have improved incredibly, my impossible dreams are still
unsolvable on the world's most powerful supercomputers. The
calculators were rapidly eclipsed by personal computers, which
themselves were eclipsed by scientific workstations which are now what
every one has on their desks. The reality of staying in business meant
that calculator development went in the direction of the needs of the
undemanding masses (note the popularity and long life of the business
calculators) and not the direction of annoying nerds with impossible
dreams.

It seems that as technology developed so as to improve what could be
built, folks could then design machines with more of a purpose, and
when that purpose was both clear and basic, there was success. One of
Bill Wickes's stated aims in developing the HP 28 was to have a machine
that provided an electronic back of an envelope for off-the-cuff
engineering calculations. This was realised superbly, but even so, it has
been discovered that for many it is still too hard to become fluent

enough so that you can really use the machine. Jeff Hawkins, with his Palm Pilot, has taken an even larger step back in that his machine is deliberately very simple (in function). It provides a basic platform on which you can build whatever you want.

To explore the longer-term future of handhelds, I would look at Japanese cellphones or Finnish mobiles. (The U.S. 'cellphone' is a synonym for 'mobile'.) These wireless phones are cheap, ubiquitous, small, have high-resolution colour screens, and access to the Internet. In evolutionary terms, this is the kind of successful form factor and simple but powerful functionality that will edge them ahead of PDAs, sub-laptops, other handhelds, and even high-end calculators. The functionality found on PDAs will slowly migrate to mobiles (and not the other way), and eventually PDAs will wither away. And yes, some of that PDA functionality would be better on a PDA than a mobile, in the same way that an HP 48 would be better on an actual HP 48 than emulated anywhere else.

I see this played out by Jeff Hawkins, who built a PDA (Palm Pilot), and then a PDA with a slot for plug-ins (Handspring). And now, of all the plug-ins that could have merged (mobile, GPS, MP3-player, digital camera, etc.) their next major device was a PDA/mobile (Treo), because it gives access to the web.

Is that your final answer?

Of course not. The reason mobiles are so popular is because people can still do what they love—prattle—and no-one has to be present. The idea of robots doing our chores never materialized; instead, every activity now comes with an ever-growing array of power tools. If ever a new handheld platform appears, it would be because some technological breakthrough allowed the creation of a hand droid that enabled us to do some task we already do, that gets us through the day, only more efficiently, easily, and effectively. The power tools will continue to exist, though they (e.g., voltmeters, torches (flashlights), GPS units, etc.) occasionally try and migrate to the handheld platform *du jour*. And perhaps we shouldn't write off those sub-laptops, since they are the embodiment of a task we do more and more of these days—sit at a computer and process.

Far more to the point is the nature of the functionality found on these hand droids. Imagine sitting down to a computer which was not connected to the internet. It would seem very small. The hand droid is connected, and probably follows the PDA model of having the basics, and you plug in your favourite toys.

Most living things, humans included, learn and grow by continually exploring and testing. Coming full circle back to the engineers and scientists, this small, mutant subset of humans tends to be overly curious, and alleviates problems with mathematics and science. Calculators enjoyed their flash of prominence because they were among the original personal computers that this mutant set so badly needed. However the other computers have evolved faster, along with the engineering problems thrown at them. The scientific calculator is retreating into its shrinking niche, out of the lab and the engineering student's classroom, into the high-school classroom.

A universal language, a standard tongue, will eventually evolve, that will be as easy to program as today's web pages, both simple and extensible. The language will undoubtedly have levels (think language, API layer, interface to platform layer, and so on) in order to make it standard on any platform. You pick up the rudiments once, rather than relearn a new language every few years (RPL, C++, Mathematica, Java, Perl, Python, XML...) to accommodate the OS flavour of the month on a machine with the shorter half-life.

I still feel very much mired in the overheads stage.

Another pint, please, waitron!

(No calculators were used in the preparation of this article.)

ABOUT THE EDITORS

Włodek Mier-Jędrzejowicz

Włodek Mier-Jędrzejowicz is a founder member of
HPCC. His interest in HP calculators began with
his studies and work in Physics at Imperial College
in London. He contributed a few early articles to
Datafile, then became the HPCC Secretary and began
writing articles regularly. This developed into a
book about the HP-41, and later books about the
HP28 and the HP-32S. He currently chairs the
club committee, continues to write for *Datafile*, and
has published a Guide to HP handheld calculators
and computers. He lives in West London surrounded by a large number
of old HP calculators. By the way, Włodek is a Polish abbreviation of
Vladimir, and you will not be surprised that he is overly fond of
Reverse Polish Notation.

Frank Wales

Frank Wales is a founder member of HPCC. He
contributed many early articles and programs to
Datafile and talked at its early conferences. As a
professional software developer, he worked on
many of Zengrange's calculator products, from
ZENROM to the *HP-41 Emulator for the HP48*, and
also worked on the tools to create them. He
recently launched his second Internet consulting
company, despite the first one still prospering. He
continues to work with, and be friends with, many
of the people he first met through HPCC. He lives in London with his
wife, Paola, and an illogical quantity of computing devices.

ABOUT THE CONTRIBUTORS

David Burch

David Burch was the spark that caused the HPCC explosion. His devotion to HP calculators began after seeing the HP35 "electronic slide-rule" demonstrated on BBC TV's *Tomorrow's World*—this led to a mad dash to HP's Heathrow warehouse to collect one of the first units to arrive in the U.K.. He wrote and edited a number of handbooks for programming tools and hardware devices such as ZENROM, ZEPROM, Zenwand and ES-41, ES-RSU, and for a number of PC software products. David is still involved in IT support for a number of small businesses, when not to be found braving the worst of the British weather in an open-top sports car.

Diana Byrne

Diana Byrne's first calculator was an HP 25, a Christmas present from her father. They spent all of Christmas vacation that year writing calculator programs. She started working at HP as a software engineer in 1987 and wrote graphing and Equation Writer code in Saturn assembly language and RPL. Diana was R&D project manager for the HP-48 G/GX and HP 38. When the HP calculator division went south (to Australia, that is) she joined Texas Instruments' calculator division in 1998. Diana has two sons. She telecommutes to Texas and lives in Corvallis, Oregon with her partner Alan, whose first calculator was also an HP-25.

Jim Carter

Jim is a Civil Engineer by training, is married to
Diane and has two daughters, Brooke and Brittany.
He lives in Modjeska Canyon in Orange County in
their dream house. It is a Geodesic Dome (actually
two domes) that Jim designed and built as the prime
contractor. Jim continues in business running
American Horse Products with Diane in the old EduCALC building in
Laguna Niguel, California.

Graeme Cawsey

Graeme starting programming HP calculators whilst
at school in the late 70's. He joined Zengrange Ltd
in 1982 as a software engineer. One of the pioneers
of assembler programming on the HP-41, he was
involved in the design and development of most of
Zengrange's HP-41 and HP-71 products, including
ZENROM, ZENWAND and ZEPROM, together with
defence and commercial systems. After Zengrange, Graeme worked for a
short time at DIP Systems in Guildford, designers of the Atari Portfolio
pocket PC. From there, he joined Grep Ltd, researching and developing
innovative systems for colour measurement and barcode scanning.
Graeme started Tuscan Consultants Ltd in 1991, developing software
and related services based around the HP95LX. Tuscan has continued to
work with Hewlett-Packard to this day, and currently provides HP's
technical support services for WindowsCE based products in the U.K..

Dave Conklin

Dave Conklin worked at HP from 1975, was on the
firmware team for the HP-41C, then became project
manager for the 41C follow-ons in 1979. After
leaving HP, he continued to develop products closely
allied to handheld computing problems, and served as
Zengrange Inc's product manager on the *HP-41*

Emulator for the HP48. Dave has a BA in mathematics from the University of California at Berkeley, and an MS degree in computer science from the University of Santa Clara. He lives in Corvallis, Oregon, and is presently working at Oregon State University on a project to model the effects on the biosphere of global climate change.

Jim Donnelly

After 16 years in calculator work, Jim now works in HP's printing business where he develops software systems to support the manufacture of inkjet-print cartridges. He lives in Oregon with his wife Jan and enjoys his machine shop and participating in community theater.

Jim Donnelly (right), with his father, Russell, who was the first person in the world to buy an HP calculator

Rabin Ezra

Rabin Ezra has been a member of HPCC for rather longer than seems strictly plausible, having become fascinated by pocket-sized devices before leaving school. As a result of spending too much time in the computer labs at university, rather than the engineering department where he should have been, he fell into a computer graphics Ph.D. and now works for Criterion Software in Guildford, England, writing the sort of code that only a 41 m-coder would find amusing.

Gary Friedman

Gary is a ten-year veteran of NASA's Jet Propulsion Laboratory, and has since gone on to found his own IT consulting firm. Perhaps his most famous invention (for which he's still trying to get funding) is the "Data Egg" typing scheme for ultra-portable devices (www.DataEgg.org). Gary also has been listed in the Guinness Book of World Records for having

built the smallest telephone (it fit into the sole of a Nike running shoe). He is the author of the book *Control the World with HP-IL*, and was a regular contributor to the *PPC Journal*, contributing mostly hardware and software projects that had the 41 and 71 computers interfacing to the outside world. Modest guy that he is, he would never mention that he is also an accomplished musician (being one of the best Xaphoon players in North America) and photographer (www.FriedmanArchives.com).

Jordi Hidalgo

When Jordi Hidalgo is not examining the back loops of pees and the crosses of tees in *Datafile*, he is programming either in C, COBOL and Visual Basic on a freelance basis, or in FOCAL, RPL and Saturn assembly, migrating applications and releasing freeware programs for his growing collection of HP handheld calculators. He lives in Barcelona, Spain.

Ron Johnson

Ron Johnson has been using HP calculators since 1973 when he bought an HP80. His current favorite calculator is the HP32SII. The 48G+, 48SX, 41CX, 41C, 30S, and more are collecting dust. Ron is a structural engineer working primarily on commercial buildings. Best calculator programming achievement:

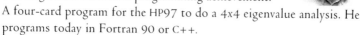

A four-card program for the HP97 to do a 4x4 eigenvalue analysis. He programs today in Fortran 90 or C++.

Neville Joseph

Neville is unusual among members in being an accountant, rather than having a technical background. He served as club chairman for a year, helped write the club's constitution, and shared his experience of running the HP BASIC User's Group. He has dabbled in politics, and has travelled to China more than once. He was an enthusiastic synthetic programming user. He lives with his wife Elna in Marlowe, Buckinghamshire, in the U.K..

Dean Lampman

Dean was a very early user of HP calculators, and he was inventor of some of the most useful early techniques of HP-65 programming, especially the technique that came to be known as 'Lampman split logic'. Since retiring, he has lectured on his experiences as an early HP user.

Richard Nelson

Richard Nelson worked in electrical engineering while he was publishing the *PPC Journal* and *CHHU Chronicle*. After ten years as Technical Support/New Products Manager at EduCALC, he continued his interests in writing as a technical writer at the Alfred Mann Foundation for Medical Research. AMF is a  Research Foundation dedicated to developing medical implant devices. Projects he has worked on include the Bionic Neuron, artificial retina, and the artificial pancreas in the writing of Patients, NIH Grants, and FDA documentation.

John Olwoch

John is one of HPCC's most prolific HP-48 programmers, and has also served on the club's committee. He joined the club after finding a second club application form inside an HP-48SX calculator box, having ignored the first one he found in an HP-41C box. He has worked at Tuscan Consultants, providing support to HP customers. He subsequently left to take an additional degree, and currently works as a software engineer. He lives in Camberley, U.K..

Mark Power

Mark Power joined HPCC in 1984 whilst studying
Computer Science. His HP-41 machine code
debugger helped towards getting a first-class degree.
Mark works for a large telecommunications company
producing software that tests a multitude of
communications equipment, and holds patents in the
use of JavaScript. Aside from the test applications
that get 1.5 million hits per day, Mark looks after the HPCC web site
that currently receives around 400 visitors per week. Mark lives in
Suffolk, England, with his wife Angie and daughter Rose, who own
respectively an HP32SII and HP71B. For therapy, he runs steam trains
around his garden.

Jake Schwartz

Jake Schwartz is a software engineer currently
working at Lockheed-Martin in southern New Jersey
in the USA. He is a long-time HP calculator
enthusiast who co-founded the Philadelphia Area HP
Handheld Club (formerly the Philadelphia–area PPC
Chapter) in 1978 with John Barnes. He participated
in various HP handheld-related activities such as attending and
presenting at calculator conferences, writing for PPC Journal, organizing
the HP41 Peripheral Routines section of the PPC ROM, beta-testing HP
products, and producing conference videotapes. Lately, his spare time
has been occupied with producing archival CD-ROM disks of the U.S.
calculator club newsletters, Hewlett-Packard handheld-related articles
and publications (i.e., HP Journal, HP Key Notes and HP Digest) and the
HPCC Datafile issues. Jake is married and has a son and two daughters.

Jeremy Smith

Jeremy Smith is a keen proponent of interactive
nomadic computing. He has contributed numerous
articles to the HP calculator clubs at meetings and in
journals, and published a reference book for the HP-
41 calculator. He emigrated from England to
America a few decades ago, where he has worked as a
computer programmer for steel, oil, environmental,

and software companies. He finally acknowledges that his birth wasn't a
mistake, but clearly, was born about a thousand years prematurely, and
would rather be beaming this note from Zepton.

Bill Wickes

Bill was an assistant professor of astronomy at the
University of Maryland, when an interest in the HP-
41C led him to write a book about synthetic
programming. This resulted in his taking a job at HP's
calculator division, where he developed many
products, including the Forth and HP-41 Translator
modules for the HP-71. He was team leader for RPL,

the HP28C/S and the HP-48SX. He is currently engaged in advanced
research for HP Laboratories' collaborative projects with academia. He
lives in Corvallis, Oregon with his wife Susan, and still has a telescope.

Raan Young

Raan Young worked as a software engineer with HP's
Corvallis/Mobile-Computing Division for 18 years
before founding his current consulting business,
Graand Visions Inc. In his alter-ego role of "Graand
Wizard", he created the da Vinci Days Kinetic
Sculpture Race (www.davinci-
days.org/schedule/ksr_race.htm) and he currently serves
on the da Vinci Days Board of Directors. He still
lives in Corvallis, Oregon, with Laura Morrison (world-reknowned

expert on wheat taxonomy and the reigning Queen of Chaos), TV the
black & white cat (now in abstentia), and far too many computers.

Additional copyright information

"A letter to PPC Journal" copyright David Burch 1982

"I blame Bill & Dave" copyright Frank Wales 2002

"The most toys" copyright Dean Lampman 2002

"Starting a calculator club" copyright Richard J. Nelson 2002

"The early years" copyright Rabin Ezra 2002

"Zengrange & John French" copyright Graeme Cawsey 2002

"A short history of EduCALC" copyright Jim B. Carter 2002

 "CHIP chapter recollections" copyright Ron Johnson 2002

"Founding the Philadelphia-area PPC Chapter" copyright Jake Schwartz 2002

"HPCC.ORG" copyright Mark Power 2002

"Why we need Datafile" copyright Jordi Hidalgo 2002

"A Really Pathetic Name" copyright Bill Wickes 2002

"HP-41 design" copyright Dave Conklin 2002

"Graphing calculator design and development" copyright Diana Byrne 2002

"Users' clubs" copyright Neville Joseph 2002

"A hardware hacker's perspective" copyright Gary Friedman 2002

"Portrait of the engineer as a young nerd" copyright Raan Young 2002

"My walk along the hall of fame" copyright Jim Donnelly 2002

"The end of an era" copyright John Olwoch 2002

"HP - There is no sequel" copyright Jeremy Smith 2002

"Constitution and name", "Datafile", "Mark Cracknell", "Conferences & meetings",
    "Gerry Rice", "Half a Beep" copyright Włodek Mier-Jędrzejowicz 2002

Index

Calculators